BE
YOUR
OWN
BOSS

BE YOUR OWN BOSS

How to Prosper in the Coming Entrepreneurial Decade

HARRY S. DENT, JR.

Published 2019 by Gildan Media LLC
aka G&D Media
www.GandDmedia.com

Front cover design by David Rheinhardt of Pyrographx

Interior design by Meghan Day Healey of Story Horse, LLC

Library of Congress Cataloging-in-Publication Data is available upon request

ISBN: 978-1-7225-0200-3

10   9   8   7   6   5   4   3   2   1

Contents

Introduction
Why You Can See the Key Economic Trends
over the Rest of Your Life Today!   7

Chapter One
The Amazing Predictive Power of Demographics
Why a Slowing Economy Is Ahead   15

Chapter Two
The Cradle-to-Grave Spending Cycle   45

Chapter Three
The Greatest Debt and
Financial Bubble in Modern History
Why It Will Burst and How You Can Prosper!   65

Chapter Four
The Four-Season Economic Model and
the Four Primary Cycles Driving It
*Why You Have to Have Different Strategies
for Each Season*   87

Chapter Five
The Direct-Marketing and Network Revolution
Four New Marketing Models and
How Network Marketing Fits In   111

Chapter Six
Options for Becoming an Entrepreneur
in This Opportune Decade Ahead
The Pros and Cons   129

Epilogue
How to Protect Your Wealth Once You've Made It   143

About the Author
151

Introduction

Why You Can See the Key Economic Trends over the Rest of Your Lifetime Today!

I am not your traditional economist. In fact I did not even get a degree in economics (thank God!). I started as an economics major but switched to accounting and finance after my first three courses.

People can't understand economists, because economists derive the opposite opinions from the same facts. Most annoyingly, they almost all claim that no one can predict the future past the next election. (I thought that that was what economics was supposed to be about.) I instead had a strong intuition that economics, like life, evolved in cycles and stages and that you could predict such cycles.

So I decided to study accounting and finance in college. After working for a Fortune 100 company for two years afterward, I went to Harvard Business School and focused on business strategy, management, and marketing. I ended up studying all aspects of business. Then I worked at Bain & Company, one of the top business-strategy consulting firms in the world, as a strategic consultant to Fortune 100 companies. I learned a lot there, especially about product life cycles and how business strategies had to change at each new stage.

I left Bain after two years, because I didn't have the patience for the slow pace of change at such large corporations. I started consulting to new ventures in California—not high-tech, but companies bringing innovations in basic consumer products and services to the young, emerging baby boom.

That's when I discovered the power of demographics.

I studied how large that generation was and how their values were different from that of the Bob Hope generation before them. I studied how their lifestyles and spending and income changed as they aged— from cradle to grave—so I could understand what they would buy and do next.

After working with innovative small businesses and poring over history for clear cycles, including delving as deeply into the consumer life cycle as I could with a whole new revolution in demographic data starting in the early 1980s, I hit my first breakthrough in 1988. I call it the *Generational Spending Wave.*

On my desk I happened to have a chart of births in the U.S. back to 1909 and a chart of the Standard & Poor 500, adjusted for inflation, over a similar time frame. The two charts looked almost identical. When I put the two together, they correlated on about a 45-year lag. That's when the light bulb went off! I already knew that the peak spending for the average household was between 45 and 49. I later found that to be age 46; now, with the millennials, it's 47.

This clear correlation of the economy and births with a 46-year lag for the peak spending of the average household told me that everyday people and businesses could see when the economy was going to boom-and-bust *almost five decades ahead*—simply by understanding their own life cycle of spending!

The truth is: you can see the key economic trends that will impact your life, your family, your business, and your investments over the rest of your lifetime. Economists can't predict such things, because they don't understand the most fundamental trends driving our economy, like new generations moving up a predictable life cycle of earning and spending.

That was 1988. In 1989 I discovered a similarly simple demographic indicator that could predict inflation decades in advance by looking at the number of new workers entering the workforce (the least productive and wealthy) versus the number of the older workers exiting (the most productive and wealthy). This affects many things, such as when bonds are good investments or not. At a more practical, everyday level, it determines how much a home mortgage or car loan is going to cost you.

Now, after over thirty years of my hard-earned research, I have developed a more comprehensive model. It combines four key cycles that can predict the key economic trends over the rest of your lifetime.

After predicting the greatest boom in history starting in 1989 in *Our Power to Predict*, I also predicted that Japan would collapse in the 1990s while the U.S. and Europe would see the greatest bull market in history. I also predicted back then, and more so in *The Great Boom Ahead* in late 1992, that the baby boom would peak in spending around 2007 and we would then face the worst economic trends of our lifetime, especially into 2020–23. Since then, I have predicted the peak of the technology and Internet bubble in early 2000 and the U.S. housing bubble in late 2005.

Now, with this much more refined model, I have *all 4 key economic cycles pointing down together from late 2019 into late 2022*, for the first time since late 1969–76 and late 1929–1934—the worst economic crises in the last century.

When I predicted the collapse of Jap S&P 500 (the Japanese equivalent of the Standard & Poor 500 index in the U.S.), everyone thought it was going to become the leading economy and overtake the U.S. I see similar downtrends for China today and for leading countries like Germany (as well as most of Europe). Demographics lets you see around the corners. Most economists simply extrapolate trends into the future. They don't understand the clearly cyclical nature of life and economics. In fact, they want to stamp out the natural cyclicality and the play of opposites that drives the very innovation that has made us so wealthy, especially in the last century. They are killing the golden goose by trying to prevent the next major downturn with unprecedented money creation and financial engineering.

Entrepreneurs and the most innovative businesses create the next great thing only when the economy faces the greatest challenges, and 2020–2023+ will be such a period!

Mark my words: There will be a huge price to pay for this economic denial and bubble, and it will arrive in the coming years, what I call the Entrepreneurial Decade. I'm here to help you turn lemons into lemonade. I am not bullish or bearish by nature. I was extremely bullish from 1988 to 2007. I am increasingly bearish from 2008 to 2023 or so. I am here to tell you the truth about economic trends and how to react accordingly.

I see the coming decade as providing the most opportunities of a lifetime, but only if you see it coming—which most won't. Entrepreneurs will do the best in this inevitable crisis ahead. I want to encourage you to become your own business in the best way suited for you.

The most important thing I bring to you is the pursuit of the truth about economics—a simple framework that you can understand and apply to your life from an independent perspective. I don't work for a major financial institution, or the government, or any political organization. I don't have a dog in the hunt. I don't have an ideology about economics. I'm not a liberal or conservative. I'm don't have a bullish or bearish bias. I just study the facts and cycles that make a difference.

This book is focused on the impacts of predictable demographic and economic cycles on the network-marketing profession. My advantage to you is that I can bring an objective and outside view precisely because I am not from this industry, nor do I have any motivation to promote or be a spokesperson for it.

I speak to any individual, investor, entrepreneur, company or industry that wants to better understand economic trends and how to better adapt to them.

In the Roaring Twenties—1925–1929—there was a bubble. There was another one, a tech bubble, in 1995–2000. We are in another great bubble. Everyone is saying this is not a bubble. But I say, if it looks like a bubble and quacks like a bubble, it is a bubble. And all bubbles burst badly throughout history, no exceptions. In chapter 4, I will cover bubbles and why it is so important to understand them NOW.

I am an entrepreneur myself. I started my own business. I have consulted for and have spoken to many entrepreneurs and have invested in many new ventures. I see challenging economic times like the 1930s, 1970s—and the decade ahead—as historically the best times for entrepreneurs. And more than ever, new Internet and social-media technologies make it easier to become an entrepreneur today.

You need to find the right approach for you if you are so inclined. This book is all about motivating you to become more serious, as the next decade could be very threatening if you don't.

The next three to four years, and possibly longer, will be the worst years for the global economy in your lifetime, as we finally get the Great Depression that we put off after 2008 with endless money printing and now tax cuts. At the same time, there are unprecedented opportunities for entrepreneurs, and for people who can generate cash, and cash flow to prosper and survive and to buy financial assets during the sale of a lifetime.

There will be clear sectors that will benefit from the aging of the massive baby-boom generation. These sectors range from health and wellness to nursing homes to home-maintenance and security and many more, which I will cover in chapter 2. The young new millennial generation will boost the demand for many products and services around raising their kids.

You will come out of this book with a better understanding of the fundamental trends that drive our economy—greater than that of the most highly educated economists. Yes, our economy is complex, but it is also very simple and very human. It is the simplest insights that allow us to see long-term trends well before they occur. You can understand such principles, and your insights will enable you to better guide your kids, invest for retirement, and manage your life and business at any level.

I will make the case that anything you can do to become an entrepreneur and increase your cash and cash flow will make you a winner in this otherwise challenging "winter" season ahead in our economy.

Read on, and I promise you will be glad you did. Best of success to you in this most difficult and opportune of times, when the cream rises to the top and entrepreneurs reign!

Chapter One

The Amazing Predictive Power of Demographics

Why a Slowing Economy Is Ahead

Most people see the economy as complex and hard to understand. You have to understand all types of supply-and-demand theories, monetary and fiscal policies, inflation and deflation, currency and exchange rates, imports and exports, trends in interest rates, productivity, and so on.

Economists spend years in school studying all types of things that most people will never understand. Yet they have a horrible track record for predicting the economy, and no one can understand them. This is because they get so caught up in the complexity and the individual indicators that they end up missing the forest for the trees.

The joke is: economists are people that aspired to be accountants, but just didn't have the personality. Don't get me wrong. Economists are some of the most educated and intelligent people you will meet. But I have found they don't measure what is most important, and they don't understand people and business—as most never have run a business themselves.

Here's the secret: *You can understand the most important trends in the economy and see the future decades out—from the growth of the economy to the growth of potato-chip sales—simply by understanding the predictable life cycle of spending for people like yourself.*

I have researched what the average household does and what they spend money on from cradle to grave from the macro side: when they create inflation and innovation, when they enter the workforce, when they earn and spend the most money, when they invest and save, when they retire, and when they die.

The most important number here is age 46: that's when the average household currently spends the most money in its lifetime. How important is that? That one number will allow you to see the booms and busts in our economy 46 years ahead (is that far enough ahead for you?). I will talk about this more later.

On the micro side, I can tell you exactly when people spend the most money on childcare, education, houses, cars, potato chips, camping equipment, life insurance, cruise ships, health care, and on and on. Or when they eat the most calories or are the tallest or weigh the most. I can explain why weight loss is one of the hottest sectors in network marketing.

The U.S. Bureau of Labor Statistics surveys over 600 categories of consumer spending every year. Just one example: the average household spends the most money on potato chips at age 42. Why? The average kid is born to the average parent when the latter is 28. Calorie intake peaks on average at age 14: 28 + 14 = 42! Even if I didn't know about the calorie and birth cycles, the consumer surveys would tell you the number is 42. If you can predict potato-chip demand decades in advance, what can't you predict?

What really drives this demographic and consumer life cycle of spending? *Generational waves of people.*

The real secret is that people are born (and immigrate, where that is a factor) in generational waves.

Everyone knows about the baby-boom generation. It's been called a pig moving through a python. This generation is the largest in modern history, and everything it does as its life cycle progresses becomes exaggerated—from baby food to sex, drugs, and rock and roll, to jeans to the housing bubble—and ahead to the greatest retirement wave and aging trends in modern history, with massive implications for our economy and for your life, business, and investments. It was further bolstered by the highest immigration rates since 1914. I adjust legal and estimated illegal immigrants into the birth chart through a computer model that uses the average age curve of immigrants, as I will discuss more just ahead.

The chart below tells the story simply. You can see 3 generations forming in the U.S. as an example if we go back as far as there are annual birth data. The Bob Hope generation peaked in births between 1921 and 1924. Even though the birth data only go back to 1909, I estimate that its birth cycle was rising from around 1897 forward. So here you have a rising tide of births from 1897 to 1924 and then a falling trend into 1933–35.

Then came the massive baby-boom generation. It was like a ten-foot wave following a three-foot wave on the beach (any surfer can tell you the difference)— it was massive. This baby boom happened around the world after World War II. It started in 1936, but

U.S. Births, 1909–2017

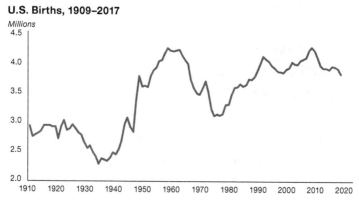

Source: U.S. Census Bureau, National Center for Health Statistics, Dent Research

was strongly up from 1937 to 1961, with a plateau top between 1957 and 1961. Some countries peaked much earlier, like Japan (in 1949), and some peaked later, like South Korea (in 1971). The U.S. peaked in 1961, Canada in 1960, Germany and most of Europe in 1964. Most developed countries had seen a peak in baby-boom births by 1971. Then the birth cycle turned down (called Generation X) from 1962 to 1973–75. The reason our economy is so slow despite massive stimulus programs is that the giant baby-boom generation has peaked in its spending cycle, and I will look at that too.

Then came the millennial generation, or what some call the *echo boom* or Generation Y. This generation has seen two surges in births. The first was from 1976 to 1990, with a 7-year downtrend into 1997. The second surge came back to similar birth levels and peaked in 2007, as I anticipated decades ago, but its impact will be muted by lower immigration trends since 2001. The millennial or echo-boom generation is larger in a small number of countries and nearly nonexistent in others, like Germany.

Births slow in cycles for two reasons. First, when the economy is unfavorable, people feel less secure and have fewer kids—duh! Note that the lowest points in births in the U.S., like 1933 and 1975, followed the worst stock crashes of the last century by one year, or more accurately, about 9 months. You do get the logic of 9 months, right? People see something scary in the economy, and 9 months later fewer babies are popping out!

Second, when a generation passes its peak child-birth years, in its late 20s, then birth rates will start to slow increasingly. That 1990 peak was baby boomers slowing in birth rates. The 2007 peak was the economy slowing down after that as a result of peak baby-boom spending and a slowing and more ominous economy and geopolitical environment. Twenty years ago, I predicted that births and immigration would decline in the U.S. after 2007.

The next generation is not likely to rise again until the early 2020s, and birth rates and immigration will not be as strong in an increasingly aging population, which has lower birth rates and more conservative political views. Although most economists and governments project births forward in straight lines, I use demographics and economic cycles to project births in a more realistically cyclical fashion.

In countries such as the U.S., Canada, Switzerland, Australia, New Zealand, and Singapore, immigration is a major factor in adding to generational cycles. These countries attract foreign immigrants who want their kids to have opportunities and get educated in English, the international language of business. They will fare the best in this downturn and even better in the upturn that eventually follows.

Here's the immigration chart for the U.S. It is even more cyclical than birth rates are. I have noted in this chart when major wars or financial depressions caused sharp declines in immigration. Since I am projecting another depression between now and 2020+, I see immigration falling further in the years ahead before the next wave hits and it is not likely to be as strong, because every other generation tends to be less open to immigration (Henry Ford and baby boom more open, Bob Hope and millennial less open).

The U.S. has been the largest immigration magnet in the world since the mid-1800s, but on a relative basis, immigration has had an even larger influence in recent decades on the demographic and generational cycles in Australia, Singapore, New Zealand, Canada, and Switzerland, in that rough order. (If Japan, South Korea, and Taiwan had this dominant English-speaking advantage, they would be immigration

U.S. Immigration Since the 1800s

Source: Department of Homeland Security, U.S. Census Bureau, Dent Research

magnets as well. Their governments should consider moving in this direction.)

When countries have large numbers of immigrants, I obviously have to add them in to make the generation waves both larger and more accurate. This can be done with a simple computer model, which takes the number of immigrants each year (legal and illegal) and then disburses them according to a predictable curve for when they were born on average. That way I take those immigrants and build them into the birth index as if they had been born here, since they now reside, work, and spend here.

That gives me what I call the *immigration-adjusted birth index*. And I make projections that follow from my birth and immigration projections out to 2060. The chart below shows what that looks like for the U.S. I have made similar adjustments for Canada and Australia, as these are the other countries where I have the most book readers and newsletter subscribers.

You can see in this chart that the level of effective births rise from a peak around 4.25 million in the birth chart previous to around 4.9 million. That's 15 percent higher, and it's a big difference. You can also see that immigrants fed a bit more into the baby boom than the millennial generation. Adjusted for immigration, the millennial generation never gets quite as high in its birth trends, although they did rival those levels in actual births. But it's important to realize that despite the hype

U.S. Immigration-Adjusted Births, 1909–2017

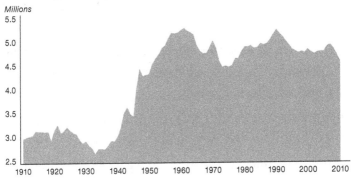

Source: U.S. Census Bureau, National Center for Health Statistics, Dent Research

about how there are more of them than boomers, the millennials are the first generation to *not* take us to new, higher levels of economic activity. For many developed countries, they take us lower. Ask Japan and Germany.

We already know when people spend the most money on almost everything. Given this fact, *the immigration-adjusted birth index creates a very powerful and fundamental tool for forecasting economic trends* in any developed country in the world decades ahead, from micro to macro levels.

This slowing and decline in generational demographic trends have profound implications for long-term economic growth, especially for housing and infrastructure. I will cover these topics in chapter 2 and in the epilogue on investing.

Now we get to the most powerful economic indicator I have ever discovered: the Generational Spending

Wave. The next chart shows the most powerful economic factor that drives the oscillating trend known as the consumer spending cycle.

The average household has a predictable life cycle of spending. For the baby boom, it started when people entered the workforce at age 20, got married at age 26, had their kid(s) at 28, and raised those kids until they left the nest when the parents were 46. Remember that I am using averages here, just as life-insurance actuaries do to predict life expectancies. Your life cycle may be a bit different, especially if you are more affluent. But note for the future: statistics in this chart show the millennial generation doing everything about a year later on average—peaking at age 47.

The kids drive this spending cycle and create the peaks. Obviously the average person does not retire at age 46 or 47. The age of 20 for entry into the workplace

Consumer Life Cycle of Spending—Millennials

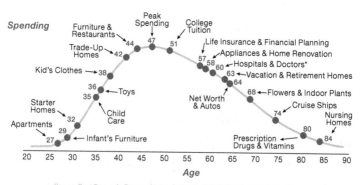

Source: Dent Research, Bureau of Labor Statistics, *Out-of-Pocket, Not Including Government Insurance

is an average of people that may enter at age 18, after high school, and others that enter at age 22, after college, or a few years later. The average kid born at age 28 (29 for millennials) is graduating from high school when the parents are at that average peak spending age of 46 (for boomers) or 47 (for millennials).

Note that there is a long plateau from around age 42, when most people have bought their largest house, to when they spend the most money on college tuition, at age 51. Then spending drops off more rapidly. The overall peak in spending for boomers, at age 46, hit in late 2007. At this point economic momentum peaked for the baby-boom generation in the U.S. (earlier in countries like Japan and later in countries in Europe and East Asia).

You can see how much we can predict from the sectors in this chart, not just the broad economy as generations age, but the big insight is that you can see the boom-and-bust cycles of our economy (and of any major country) by simply moving forward the immigration-adjusted birth index 46 years (for boomers) or 47 years (for millennials) to find the predictable peak in spending of the average household. I call this the Generational Spending Wave.

Here's the Generational Spending Wave for the U.S. It correlated closely with the stock market (adjusted for inflation) until 2009, when the Federal Reserve and global central banks started printing $17 trillion to goose up stocks. That won't last after the next crash brings our economy back to normal. The U.S. is the best country to prove this concept, as it is the largest economy in the world and one of the most self-sufficient. Our exports and imports are only about 12 percent of our economy, whereas many countries, like Germany or South Korea, have exports as high as 50 percent of GDP. China's is more like 35 percent. For countries with high exports, their trading partners can determine their growth substantially beyond their own internal demographic trends. Even so, I can predict the demographic trends in any major country around the world, even in emerging countries like China, Malaysia, Indonesia, India, Brazil, and Kenya.

I discovered this incredibly simple correlation between births and peak spending in 1988. Simultaneously I predicted the greatest boom and bull market in history for the 1990s for the U.S. and Europe, along

U.S. Generational Spending Wave—Turned Down 2008–2023
Births Lagged for Peak Spending vs. The Real Dow

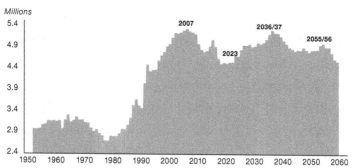

Source: Dent Research, U.S. Census Bureau, Bloomberg

with the collapse of Japan. Who else saw both of those things coming?

Even back then I was predicting that the U.S. economy would peak around late 2007. Then demographic trends would slow, and we would see a long downturn from 2008 into 2020–23. That's why such massive stimulus from governments has had such a weak impact on the economy. In chapter 3 I'll look at the greatest debt bubble in history and why that is weighing on nearly all economies around the world.

With my projections for the immigration-adjusted birth index, I can project trends out to 2060 (and farther out, using some simple assumptions) in any major country in the world. As I promised in the introduction, you can see the key economic trends that will impact your life, your business, your family, and your investments over the rest of your lifetime, and even over the lifetimes of your kids and grandkids.

A few things to explain here: This peak in spending has advanced over time. The Bob Hope generation peaked at age 44 on average, the baby boom at age 46. The millennials are already looking to peak at age 47 for the first wave (born up to 1990), and likely at age 48 for the second surge, which peaked in 2007. I adjust the lag over time.

In Japan and East Asian countries like South Korea, Taiwan and Singapore, as well as in most European countries, I find that the peak is closer to 47, which is likely to mean age 48 going forward. This is due to the higher immigration in the U.S., which causes the peak to be a little lower, as education levels tend to be lower for immigrants, which delays peak spending.

The more affluent you are, the later your peak in spending. More affluent people tend to go to school longer and enter the workforce later; their kids tend to go to school longer before they leave the nest. The most affluent households, the college-educated, the top 20 percent, peak around age 51, not 46 or 47. That's when spending on college tuitions peaks. Recent payroll surveys have shown that full-time college-educated workers don't peak until age 57, and that was in late 2018.

Since 2008 the average household in the U.S. has seen its spending cycle turn down. But this did not occur for the most affluent, college-educated, full-time professionals, who, at age 57, are the last segment to peak after 2018. These people have still been spending and have most benefited from the government money-printing programs that have filtered into bubbling stock markets, even though the economy has been mediocre. When these people stop spending—from 2018 forward—look out, especially in 2020 or 2021 at the latest!

Let's turn back to the chart of the consumer life cycle of spending on page 24. There are important transitions. First, we have to be born to become consumers, and that doesn't happen without sex. So I always say that it's actually sex that drives our economy (and that's why economists have never figured it out!).

From the time we are born until we enter the workforce, we are an expense—or a better way to put it is that parents invest in raising their kids, and that investment pays off when they enter the workforce and become productive citizens. This insight allows us to understand inflation in simple human terms:

Kids cost everything and produce little or nothing: young people are the greatest driver of inflation, and we can predict their impact on inflation trends and interest rates decades in advance.

The greatest inflation in modern history happened when the pig in the python, the baby boomers, was peaking in entering the workforce. It takes about $250,000 to raise the average kid through high school in the U.S. for the average household, then for many, there's college. Governments fund much of the education system, so they invest in young people as well. Then businesses hire young people after school and have to invest in offices, equipment, and training.

One year after I discovered the Generational Spending Wave in 1988, I found an astounding correlation with workforce growth, on a 2.5-year lag, and inflation. See the chart on page 30.

Obviously a lot of things that can affect the inflation rate: swings in the economy; currency exchange rates, which make imported products cheaper or more

Inflation Indicator and Forecast
The Consumer Price Index vs. Workforce Growth on a 2.5-year lag

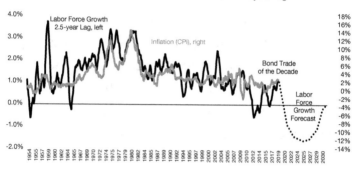

Source: Bureau of Labor Statistics, Dent Research

expensive; swings in oil and food prices; wars; monetary policies; budget deficits; and so on. But the correlation of this one factor proves that this is not a just *a* factor; it is the driving factor. This correlation was mind-boggling when I discovered it in 1989, almost as much as the Generational Spending Wave in 1988.

Workforce growth is high when a lot of young people are entering, as with the peak years for the baby boom from 1977 to 1981 (a twenty-year lag on peak births from 1957 to 1961). Inflation rates peaked in the U.S. in 1980. It also slows when a lot of people retire, as the boomers increasingly will from 2020 to 2024. The 2.5-year lag on workforce entry clearly shows that it takes that long for the typical new worker to finally produce more than they cost in training and equipment.

The great thing is that we can predict inflation trends decades ahead by projecting the number of people that will enter the workforce at age 20 on average and the number that will retire at age 63 on average.

Older countries have lower inflation, like Japan and increasingly Europe and East Asia in the years ahead. Inflation has been near zero for over two decades in Japan, as it is the most rapidly aging country in the world (there has even been deflation). Germany and Europe have seen very low inflation rates, as they are aging faster than the U.S. or East Asian countries. Young countries, especially developing countries, have higher inflation.

The trend in the developed world is increasingly towards deflation, not inflation, despite massive government money printing and stimulus programs to counteract such deflation. Investors and businesses in wealthier, developed countries from Europe to East Asia have to plan more on deflation than inflation, on slower growth rather than on faster growth.

It would appear to be common sense to see governments printing money at an unprecedented and even reckless rate and think, "That's got to cause inflation, maybe even hyperinflation—I better buy some gold!" That is not what you should do. *Creating cash and cash flow is the best way to prosper in deflationary times.* That's what entrepreneurs do best. This is an opportunity that network marketing offers. I will give more summary investment recommendations in the epilogue.

Entering the workforce is the next big phase of the consumer life cycle, as we become productive citizens that earn, spend, and become increasingly productive, expanding the economy. This is what causes booms like those from 1942 to 1968 and from 1983 to 2007. The rising productivity of people from 2.5 years after they enter the workforce (age 22.5 for the average person) drives inflation down. Not only were the 1970s the decade with the highest inflation rates in modern history, they were also the lowest decade for productivity rates, because baby boomers were not yet fully in the workforce (and were largely still in school) and were weighing on the economy with their costs.

Then comes age 46 (for baby boomers), when the average person peaks in their spending. At that point, their kids are getting out of school, leaving the nest (hopefully), and getting jobs on their own. The parents' expenses drop dramatically, which allows them to start to save for retirement. Since 2007 we have seen the lowest real GDP growth rates since 1929–40 (19 percent cumulative versus 20 percent cumulative back then), which is due to boomers (predictably) spending less. It would have been much worse without massive money printing, which kept stock markets, real estate, and financial assets much higher than they would have been, making at least the older and more affluent a lot richer. Hence we go into a saving phase, when spending goes down and net worth expands dramatically. Net worth peaks for the average household at age 64, one year after retirement.

Finally comes retirement, on average at age 63, when the household spends down its net worth, and people stop working partially or fully and continue to downsize until death.

A good way to summarize these key stages of life is in the chart above. The generation first goes through a wave of innovation and inflation as they peak in workforce entry and learning at around age 22.5 (age 20 for entry, plus 2.5 years to start earning more than they cost to their employers).

This is a stage of education and innovation. It is young people coming out of college at age 22 that most drive new technologies and new consumer trends. Young people may cost a lot, but their payoff at this stage is their innovation. They try new things. Older people just get more entrenched in what they already

Generational Waves and Transitions

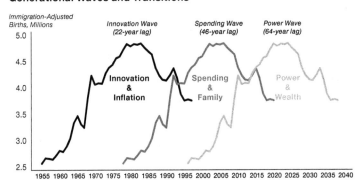

Source: U.S. Census Bureau, National Center for Health Statistics. Dent Research

know or like. Early on I found a correlation with small-cap stocks—companies that are typically more innovative and enjoy higher growth—and a 22-year lag on the immigration-adjusted birth index for these new, higher-end, and college-educated workers. Large-cap stocks like the Dow and S&P 500 correlate with the Generational Spending Wave.

The next phase is the spending and productivity cycle, which generates long-term booms in the economy. During this boom in spending, the rising generation has the money to adopt and purchase the innovations they generated earlier. Their rising productivity brings inflation back down again. That obviously peaks at age 46. It hit in 2007 for the massive baby-boom generation, with the Great Recession to follow from 2008 into 2009. Ever since, we have seen massive stimulus combined with mediocre growth.

The same has been true for the Japanese since late 1996, when their Generational Spending Wave started to peak, way ahead of those of the U.S. and Europe. Most of Europe is next to fall, with Germany having the worst demographic trends of any country in the world between 2015 and 2022; it is second only to Japan in its rate of aging of its population (and everyone is looking for Germany to hold up the European Union)! South Korea will be the last wealthy country to fall off this demographic cliff after 2018 (apart from Spain, which is already in a depression from the aftermath of a massive real-estate bubble).

In my 2014 book, *The Demographic Cliff*, I address in more depth how this demographic decline after baby-boom peaks will continue to cascade around the world, hitting one country and region after the next. But the next chart summarizes the trends in the wealthiest countries around the world, where network marketing is concentrated:

In summary, there are six smaller countries that actually have larger millennial or echo-boom generations than the baby boom. I call these wealthy countries the *gainers*. These countries have higher growth ahead after the global downturn and depression I see up to 2020–22. They are, in rough order, Australia, Singapore, Switzerland, Norway, Sweden, and New Zealand.

The countries that have millennial generations that are nearly the size of their baby booms are what I call

Gainers, Sustainers & Decliners
Demographics Tell the Tale

GAINERS		
Australia	Israel	New Zealand
Norway	Singapore	Sweden
SUSTAINERS		
Canada	Denmark	France
Switzerland	United Kingdom	United States
DECLINERS		
Austria	Belgium	China
Finland	Germany	Greece
Italy	Japan	Netherlands
Portugal	Russia	South Korea
Spain	Taiwan	Eastern Europe
The rest of the developed world		

the *sustainers*. They will see slower and/or more buoyant growth even in the next global boom, and they will grow more from productivity than from demographics. These are larger countries like the U.S., France, the U.K., Canada, Switzerland, and Denmark (which, by the way, has been often rated as the happiest country in the world).

The hard truth is that most developed countries will now or later become *decliners*. These include Japan, Taiwan, South Korea (after 2018), Germany, Austria, Greece, Italy, Portugal, Spain (after 2025), most of Eastern Europe, and Russia (including all of the former Soviet Union, such as Ukraine and Georgia). In the emerging world, they will even include mighty China.

Around the world, *demographic trends get worse over the next several years, not better.* More countries will fall off the demographic cliff, following Japan in the 1990s and the U.S. after 2007. Most have declining demographic trends for decades—including Japan, Germany, and China. Governments that think we are over this economic slowdown are in for a rude awakening, likely starting in 2020. (More on this in chapters 3 and 4.)

Finally, the generation hits its phase of power and wealth in the professions, management, and government, from age 47 to the point where these people retire at age 63. The top management of most companies (as well as government officials) are not in their 20s; they are in their 50s and 60s. The baby boom has been in this phase since 2008, and it will last to 2025.

This generation reaches a peak of net worth at age 64. After that it fades into the sunset as the next generation, the millennials, will be ascending in their spending wave. The baby boom in the U.S. will die in increasing numbers from 2017 to around 2043. (This assumes their life expectancy will grow from 79 today to 82 by then; it could grow faster. I will be able to monitor and adjust for that.)

This trend will have huge implications for real estate and infrastructure, because for the first time in modern history, there are more diers than buyers. This trend began back in 2006 for Japan and will come a bit later in one country after the next in the developed world.

You should also be aware that the U.S. government's forecasts for population growth are way off. They project births and immigration going up in straight lines from the very favorable trends of recent decades. With my more realistic and cyclical projections, I estimate the U.S. population will grow at a mere 0.28 percent a year, to 360 million by 2060. The government projects 420 million. That's 60 million people that simply won't be there. Because of this aging trend, real estate will never be the same, as I discuss in depth in chapter 3 of *The Demographic Cliff.*

I have looked at population trends in Canada and Australia for my newsletter subscribers there. The

Canadian government is projecting 52 million people by 2060; I am projecting 42 million. That's a huge difference. Australia is projecting 42 million; I am projecting 35 million. Australia will have demographic and population growth that, even at my lower estimates, that will be the envy of the developed world, as will Singapore, Israel, and New Zealand. These countries (except Israel) depend more on immigration than on births for growth, and immigration will continue to fall sharply in the greatest downturn since the Great Depression ahead. But all countries are projecting straight-line and ever higher birth rates, whereas births will fall in an economic downturn. Don't believe the population-growth projections of any developed country.

In chapter 6 of *The Demographic Cliff*, I also look at the enormous and increasingly dominant demographic trends in the emerging world—from Asia to South America to the Middle East to Africa. These countries are most driven by increasing urbanization, which tends to double or triple incomes and spending—something the developed countries have already accomplished.

It is an illusion that the emerging countries will become as rich as the developed ones. The richest today is Malaysia, with 77 percent urbanization and $31,216 GDP per capita PPP (purchasing-power parity, that is, adjusted for cost of living), versus $56,000 in the U.S. and $40,000+ in most of the developed world. How much richer are Malaysians going to be when they reach 80 percent-plus urbanization? I project $34,500 GDP per capita PPP at 85 percent urbanization in 2026 for Malaysia: only 60 percent of that the U.S. Nevertheless, it is a rare example of an emerging country that has entered the lower rung of the living standards of developed countries.

China has $18,369 GDP at 59 percent urbanization. This is projected to grow to as high as $27,000 when (like Malaysia) it reaches 85 percent around 2045. That's still a bit less than 50 percent of the GDP of the U.S. today. That's as good as it gets, unless you become a high-end manufacturer and financial-services provider, like Japan, South Korea, Taiwan, and Singapore. Only so many countries in the world can do that, just as only so many people can be affluent beyond middle-class living standards, even in the richest countries.

Then there is the low end, with a country like Kenya. It's at only $3,476, with 28 percent urban. Sometime in the next century, at 85 percent urban, its GDP is only projected to be $7,200. That's only 13 percent of that of the U.S. today. The average for emerging countries today is $12,525 GDP per capita PPP, versus $51,573 for developed countries. So today the developed nations are just over four times richer.

Even so, these emerging countries have almost all of the demographic and urbanization growth potential in the world ahead. For peak spending, the demographic and spending trends in these countries follow workforce growth more closely than they do the 46–47-year lag, as the incomes of these nations do not surge as much with age as those of the developed countries with age. Workforce growth is also easy to project decades into the future, so I have similar spending waves out to 2060 for emerging countries.

To summarize here: China's demographic growth peaked in 2011 and will decline in the decades ahead, especially after 2025, but it is still only 59 percent urban. It will benefit from increasing urbanization after it works off the greatest real-estate and government-driven infrastructure bubble in modern history (that could take 5–10 years). That means it will likely come out of the great financial crisis ahead much more slowly than the rest of the emerging world.

China could see the greatest bust of all major countries in the world, because of its unprecedented bubble in real estate and urbanization, which will burst in the decade ahead. China is the greatest government-driven bubble in urbanization, infrastructure, and real estate in all of modern history. It is also the only emerging country that, like much of the developed world, has declining demographic and workforce-growth trends for decades ahead. The inevitable bursting of its bubble burst will make it the epicenter of the next financial crisis.

But China will boom again from the mid- to late 2020s forward, just at lower rates than in the past three decades of unprecedented growth. China and India have the largest new middle-class populations that could become fertile ground for many industries, including network marketing.

India is the largest emerging country, with some of the strongest demographic trends and urbanization potential, as it is only 34 percent urban. Southeast Asia and India will boom demographically into around 2055 before plateauing and slowing down. South America is already urbanized and will grow more slowly, with rising demographic trends into around 2040, with Mexico as its rising star in manufacturing exports.

The Middle East and North Africa will grow very rapidly if they ever get out of their civil wars. (I expect these to settle out in the early 2020s, as I will discuss more in chapter 4, where I show a very powerful geopolitical cycle.) Sub-Saharan Africa has the most potential for growth from both demographic trends and urbanization, but this region largely hasn't joined the capitalist party yet, and it is still plagued by massive corruption and poverty. It will be the last to urbanize and grow more effectively.

Despite massive demographic and urbanization potential, the emerging world will not continue to advance and see its day in the sun until commodity prices stop falling on a predictable 30-year cycle, which peaked in 2008, and until the developed world goes through its debt and financial crisis (between 2020 and

2023 or so). These countries depend heavily on exports to the developed world and tend to have worse downturns than ours despite stronger demographic trends—but when they recover, they will dominate growth from the early 2020s forward.

Entrepreneurs Thrive in Downturns

I have just explained, using the simplest logic ever, the most important driving trend for our economy in the modern middle-class world—which really did not exist before World War II. Most people and most industries like a boom and don't do as well in a bust. The two big, long-term bust periods before 2008 were 1930–42 and 1969–82, as the Generational Spending Wave would have forecast decades before those downward demographic trends set in. The next is 2008–22.

Note that the unprecedented money printing and stimulus to stave off the Great Recession and financial meltdown of 2008–09 will make this long phase of downturn and depression the opposite of the Great Depression of 1930–42. There we saw the worst crash and unemployment right off the bat after the dramatic 89 percent 1929 stock crash. Then there was a recovery into 1937 and there was an aftershock in 1937–38, with a deep recession that lingered into 1942.

This time around, we had the Great Recession, which was muted by the unprecedented QE (quantitativeeasing, that is, money-printing) program. That merely pushes off the great deleveraging, which clears debt and inefficiencies out of the economy, making it healthier to move forward again. Hence we will see the greatest depression and stock crash on the back side of this winter season, from 2020 to 2023 or so. Then the next global boom will start around 2023–24, from demographic trends that will be much weaker in most of the developed world; this time they will be dominated by the emerging countries.

In these down periods, when unemployment goes up, most businesses slow or decline, and stocks crash for many years on and off. But entrepreneurs shine! While most larger businesses are stumbling and restructuring and being forced into efficiency, entrepreneurs and entrepreneurial companies take advantage of the changes and opportunities that emerge. This coming decade will usher in a new era for entrepreneurs.

I heard a speaker say that more millionaires were made in the Great Depression than in any other time in history (relative to population, of course). Most of the great growth companies in our boom from 1983 to 2007 were entrepreneurial startups in the downturn from 1969 to 1982, from Apple to Home Depot and zillions of other companies.

The challenging decade ahead will be a great opportunity for the more innovative people to start or become their own companies—from aging baby boomers, who want to have more control over their destiny as they age, to younger millennials, who see less and less opportunity for getting good jobs as unemployment soars beyond anyone's expectations. I will address the broader spectrum of entrepreneurial opportunities in chapter 5.

In chapter 2 I will look at the cradle-to-grave spending cycle and at how you can see when individual consumer sectors will boom and bust decades in advance—just as we can for the overall economy.

The great thing about demographics is that there is always something booming, even if the general economy is not. And it is the entrepreneurs that are most likely to find those opportunities, especially if they understand the predictive power of demographics.

Chapter Two

The Cradle-to-Grave Spending Cycle

The most exciting trends for all ranges of entrepreneurs will come from the sectors that will continue to grow from the aging of the baby boomers, even though their overall spending will decline as they save for retirement. There will also be new trends as the slightly smaller and younger millennial generation continues to enter the workforce and advance into their family cycle.

Before I get into the why, I am going to start this chapter with the top nine consumer sectors for growth from the aging baby boomers in the coming decade plus (after the economic decline I see into 2020–23):

1. Discretionary health and wellness: vitamins, antiaging, and skin care
2. Pharmaceutical drugs and disease treatment
3. Home art and decoration (no longer major renovations)
4. Cruise ships
5. Convenience stores and drugstores
6. Security and control systems
7. Pest and termite control
8. Funeral and cremation services
9. Nursing homes and assisted-living facilities

The millennial generation will also see a major surge in sectors that revolve around having and raising kids—from childcare to kids' clothes to furniture and family restaurants. In real estate, millennials will be looking to move out of rentals, first into affordable starter homes, with easier-to-access and lower-cost financing; then, after 2025, they will increasingly be looking for trade-up homes, into the latter stages of their boom into 2036–37.

In Japan, which saw its baby-boom generation peak between late 1989 and late 1996 (way ahead of those of most developed countries), adult diapers now outsell baby diapers. Holy crap, Batman! Is this a sign of a major shift or what?

Here's the key insight: since the baby boom is the largest generation in almost all developed countries, and more importantly, it has the steepest growth curves for every consumer sector it enters, the best growth markets will come from the areas where boomers will spend more as they move into their 65–80+ age ranges in the next global boom from 2023 into 2036–37.

A great thing about demographics is that we can predict the trends in nearly all key consumer sectors, down to potato chips, with the same tools as we predict trends in macro spending, borrowing, investing, and inflation.

As in the example of potato chips I gave in chapter 1, if the peak in that sector is age 42, then you can simply move the immigration-adjusted birth index 42 years forward, rather than 46 for the overall economy. Potato chips would have peaked around 2003 on that lag. For cruise-ship travel, which now peaks at age 74, this sector will grow and will not peak until around 2035. For nursing homes, the peak will be the latest, at 2045+.

The simplest way to think about microtrends in consumer segments is to take the peak of the baby-boom births in 1961 (for the U.S.) and add the age for the peak in spending for that sector. Cruise ships: 1961 peak births + age 74 peak = 2035 peak for industry.

The same goes for the up-and-coming millennial generation. It is far from being fully incorporated into the workforce (this will not happen until around 2028), and it is much farther from its peak spending in 2055–

56. Its first wave of births peaked in 1990. The second wave came in 2007. Another quick example, for people making money buying cheap houses or apartments and renting them out: apartment rentals peak at age 27. That means demand for the first wave would peak around 2017 (1990 + 27 = 2017, and for the second, in 2035–36 (allowing for a slightly later future marriage age, at 29). In the near term, this sector is likely to peak a bit later, because the economy is so soft and home buying is more difficult and seems riskier (and it is, and it will get worse).

You obviously get a better picture of the trends over time if you graph out the lag for peak spending in that or any sector on the immigration-adjusted birth index. I will give some examples ahead.

The only other caveat is that you have to consider to what degree the ups and downs of the general economy (on the 46-year Generational Spending Wave) will impact spending in any consumer sector. In the case of potato chips, a down economy would have only minor impacts on spending. For big-ticket items like houses or cars, the impact would be higher. In the network-marketing arena, the impact on travel would likely be a bit greater than on health and wellness.

I also have simple demographic forecasts for inflation, which impacts interest rates. Rising and falling interest rates affect some sectors more than others, notably housing and cars. They do impact returns on investments for financial advisors and the costs and benefits from life insurance. They don't significantly affect health care or travel.

THREE SNAPSHOTS OF THE CONSUMER-SPENDING LIFE CYCLE

Let me walk through the consumer life cycle in more detail. At Dent Research, we have hundreds of categories of consumer spending tracked by age. It is condensed in a research report entitled *Spending Waves* (at dentresearch.com). I am going to review the more pertinent areas, first in consumer spending and then in real estate, as we are dealing not just with one sector, but with a series of very different purchases over our life cycle.

The first chart looks at some of the key sectors in the earlier phase, after we enter the workforce. At

The Family Stage of the Consumer Spending Cycle

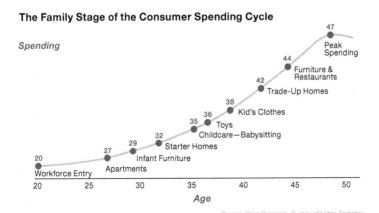

Source: Dent Research, Bureau of Labor Statistics

this point, we are raising our families and buying our houses. The first car used to come at age 26, just before or at the average age of marriage (I'm assuming a guy has to get a car to get a girl here; at any rate, that used to be the case). But not with millennials. They Uber more until they have kids, then auto buying accelerates at around age 29. Apartments peak at 27, as married couples start looking to buy a house as soon as they can afford it and/or have kids, which occurs at age 29 on average (and rising in the future). Cribs and baby furniture first, then childcare, and then the infant-clothing surge.

Starter-home buying peaks around age 32 for millennials. Around that are a lot of furnishings—think home developers and IKEA booming here. This is huge stimulus to the economy. It was the key factor behind the strong growth of the 1980s boom and the savings-and-loan bubble, which burst in the early 1990s. Childcare and babysitting peak at age 35, just as that average kid finally goes to school and the parents get a break.

Kindergartens peak for one year at age 34, then elementary schools boom from age 35 to 41, then high schools, from age 42 to 47. Looking back, I was startled that they didn't build schools fast enough for the baby boomers, and then they overbuilt just when the baby boomers were graduating out of that level. What could be more obvious and predictable?

The next big jolt for the economy comes when people buy their largest or trade-up home between the ages of 38 and 42. Mortgage interest peaks at age 42 to confirm this. That trend towards McMansions for the boomers should have peaked around 2002, but the housing bubble took it all the way through 2005 with unprecedented speculation.

People don't buy their largest house at age 47, when they have the most income and highest spending; they buy that house when their kids turn into nasty, hormonal teenagers. After all, 42 (peak for the millennials) minus 29 (age at birth of kid) = 13! You (and they) want more space to be as far from one another as possible. Furniture and eating out at family restaurants also peak at age 44, just after that peak home purchase, and ahead of the overall peak in spending at age 47, which begins the midlife stage of life and spending.

The Mid-Life Stage of the Consumer Spending Cycle

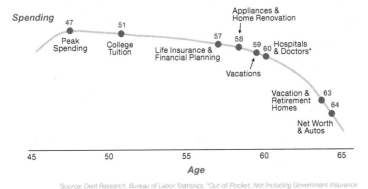

Source: Dent Research, Bureau of Labor Statistics. *Out-of-Pocket, Not Including Government Insurance

The parents continue to spend money on education, for those that go to college, and on cars and tires to cart the kids around into age 47, when the total peak in spending occurs. That's because a majority of kids don't go to school past, or much past, high school. The parents are age 47 on average, when those kids turn 18 and graduate.

At this point the parents have bought that big house and furnished it. They are seeing their kids start to leave or at least get a job and start to support themselves. This is what creates the midlife crisis and leads to a new lifestyle of travel and entertainment. What do we do now that we don't have to spend all our money and time on the kids and on building and furnishing the house?

Men get motorcycles (this peaks around age 48), then sports cars, luxury cars, boats, and country clubs, which peak by ages 53–54. Women spend more money on clothes, entertaining, and home improvement in this time period. People start to travel more. That doesn't peak until age 59 for normal trips and vacations away from home, but people switch to hassle-free cruise ships into age 74. (That number was age 70 for the boomers and may continue to rise.) If you're going to buy a vacation home, this is the first surge into around age 48, and it doesn't peak until age 63. A vacation home is a good place for leisure, but it's also for attracting the kids, and later grandkids, to come back and see you now and then.

For the more affluent or for households who have kids who go to college, tuition peaks at age 51 (likely 52 in the future as the millennials move into that stage). These more affluent households have kids a little later, so it's not surprising that this peaks here. As I mentioned in chapter 1, the top 20 percent of more affluent households peak in their spending around 51, not ages 46–47. They go to school longer, and typically so do their kids.

The splurge on autos—for yourself, not for a boring minivan to cart your kids around—used to peak at age 50 for boomers, but now peaks at age 64, along with their net worth, and then falls off steeply. And it's not because they are trading down in quality. I can always tell when I'm buying a car from an older person. It will have 50,000 miles on it and be 10 years old. If I'm buying it from a soccer mom, it will have 80,000 miles on it and be 4 years old. Older people do not have to cart their kids around all day to school, soccer practice, the dentist, or Ecstasy parties. They just go down to Starbucks, get a coffee and a paper, and come back home and take a nap. Older people simply don't drive nearly as many miles, and they keep their cars longer. That's why sales used to plummet after age 50, and now after 64.

Automobiles, along with big-ticket homes, could be the worst industry to suffer when the great crash and depression ahead hit. On top of boomers not feeling so rich late in life, millennials aren't buying cars as much—they Uber more.

Since the 2009 crash bottom, middle-age people have gotten rich off the stock and real-estate bubble created by massive money printing through QE. Car sales are now peaking at age 64, just after retirement at age 63. But I predict this will not last when these great bubbles burst, likely between 2020 and 2022. Cars will likely go back to peak spending around age 50–51, when kids graduate from college and free up parents' discretionary income.

In this midlife crisis, people start leaving the workforce, especially women in two-earner families. Now that the kids are through college (especially for more affluent households), both no longer have to work, and more women will be looking for part-time work, which can be more fulfilling and more flexible from the home.

People start doing more financial planning for retirement. This is marked by life insurance and annuities peaking at age 57.

Couples and divorcees also get into entertainment after their kids leave the nest, especially women. This is where people spend the most money on home improvement—renovated kitchens and bathrooms, pools and patios, china and dinnerware, wine cellars, and so on. Major home appliances and capital improvements to homes both peak around age 58, and that was in 2019 for the boomers. This is another set of industries that will suffer strongly from the great crash of 2020–22+.

Out-of-pocket spending on doctors and hospitals peak around age 60, as more people get on Medicare and Medicaid.

When Cruises Peak

Let me give an example of how I project forward for peak spending in a sector, just as I do for the overall economy. So let's look one of the sectors mentioned above that continue to grow past the late 50s. Overall travel grows until age 59–60, which means that for boomers it will peak by 2020–21—not far away.

So . . . why not go on a cruise ship? Just stuff me with food and booze and I'll be happy—no changing hotel rooms, no customs, no jet lag. Cruise ships don't peak until age 74. That is a growth market all the way out to 2035 or so (on a 74-year lag on births!). And this chart keeps advancing later in life over time.

Cruise Ship Spending by Age—Peaks at Age 74
Average Annual Spending by Age, Indexed to 20-Year-Olds, 2008–2016

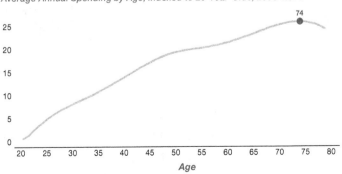

Source: Dent Research, Bureau of Labor Statistics

The joke in the cruise-ship industry is "we attract the newlywed and the nearly dead." That is an exaggeration, but you can see the progression in this chart. The first surge is newlyweds into age 25–26. Then there is steady growth into age 46 from family and kids and teenagers. From age 50–60 there is the peak surge from empty-nest households, who are traveling more. But the strongest surge by far comes from age 63–74, when this becomes the final easy travel option for older people in retirement. Since this peak has already moved from age 70 to 74 in the last decade, it could continue to move later in life ... right up until the boomers step into the nursing home.

Cruise Ships Don't Peak Until 2035+
U.S. Immigration-Adjusted Births Moved Forward 74 Years

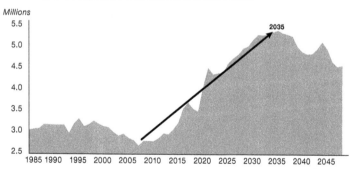

Source: U.S. Census Bureau, National Center for Health Statistics, Dent Research

This is an example of how you can get a clearer view of trends over time from simply lagging the immigration-adjusted birth index forward for the peak in spending of any particular consumer sector.

The Retirement Stage of the Consumer Spending Cycle

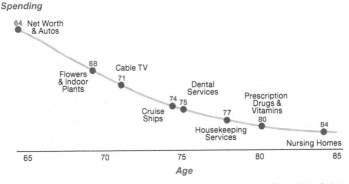

Source: Dent Research, Bureau of Labor Statistics

Now let's look at the last stage, retirement.

In this phase, health issues become strong again. Medicare copayments peak at age 79. Prescription drugs don't peak until age 80. I consider this a close proxy to vitamins and antiaging and wellness products, which are not covered in the Consumer Expenditures Survey. However, I was able to find a good chart on vitamins and supplements (see next page), which looks even more favorable.

Note that this chart shows age segments in smaller time frames in childhood, then in 10-year segments afterwards. There is a surge in vitamins and supplements into age 5, when kids have the most childhood challenges and diseases. Then the trends turn up the most sharply from age 20 to 29, which will be a hot area for 2015–20 from rising millennials, but this arena keeps going up into the age 80+ age range for baby boomers—just like pharmaceuti-

Supplement Use by Age—Peaks at Age 80+ Like Pharmaceuticals
Prevelance of Supplement Usage, females

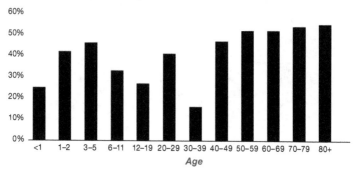

Source: National Health and Nutrition Examination Survey

cals. Note that this chart is for women, who are 20 percent more likely to consume supplements than men—hence they are better customers and distributors—although the age trends for men are similar.

Vitamins and antiaging and health and wellness products have many sectors that never peak until death or near death. That means growth into the early 2040s for the boomers. But the up-and-coming millennial generation will continue to add impetus to this trend from 2015 forward.

Among the hottest recent areas has been weight loss. (I could have guessed that from watching Marie Osmond on every other commercial on TV!) I researched for more insights into why, and I found this chart on weight by age (see next page).

People weigh the most at around age 60. That means a growth market into around 2021—not very far

Body Weight Peaks at Age 60 Driving Weight Loss Surge into 2021
Median of Men and Women

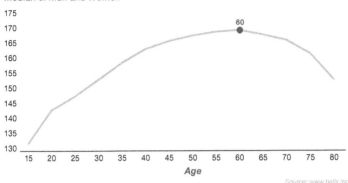

Source: www.halls.md

ahead. Note that women drop off more steeply, but men stay nearly as heavy into age 70, so the market for them stays strong into at least 2031. Couples who divorce in midlife after their family cycle is over will also become more weight-conscious in their 50s.

Just a side comment here to reinforce the importance of demographics beyond spending and other economic factors. What *don't* aging and our life cycle impact? We're born 9 months after sex, our brain grows and wires the most in the first 5–6 years, we consume the most calories at age 14, we are the tallest at age 18–19 (actually our heights can be largely predicted at age 2), we have the highest cognitive abilities at age 50, we weigh the most at age 60, we are the happiest around age 63–64, when we retire and have the highest net worth . . . then we die.

I'll end with an illustration of the ultimate growth industry for the next three decades: nursing homes

Nursing Home Spending by Age—Peaks Last at 84
Average Annual Spending by Age, Indexed to 20-Year-Olds

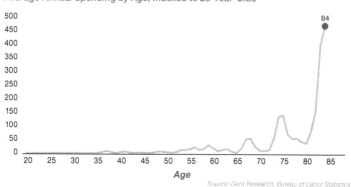

Source: Dent Research, Bureau of Labor Statistics

and assisted-living centers. The graph above shows that peak between 80 and 84. Yes, this industry will grow until around 2045, longer than I will live, as I will be one those baby boomers dying before then.

This is my number-one sector for growth in the next global boom. It will be the last to capture the full growth phase of the baby boomers from 2019 to 2045, when we lag forward for 84 years. In addition, nursing homes are often too expensive and do not offer prompt or customized service when clients have needs and problems. Digital sensors could solve a lot of those problems. Many millionaires will be made in the local sectors of assisted living and nursing homes. People like Gene Guardino at Residential Assisted Living Academy, based in Phoenix, are teaching people how to turn homes into such mini assisted-living centers and generate high cash flow and higher home

Demand For Nursing Homes Will Explode 2019–2045
U.S. Immigration-Adjusted Births Moved Forward 84 Years

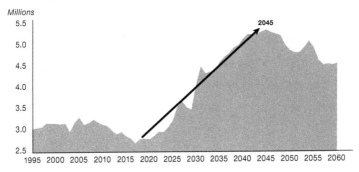

Source: U.S. Census Bureau, National Center for Health Statistics, Dent Research

values from the unique facilities improvements for this aging sector. But some billionaires will be made from companies that can franchise or build much larger regional, national, or global solutions.

I've given some of the more important and obvious examples here for sectors that should expand the most with aging boomers. The simplest way to look at the coming boom and decade is: what will boomers most need in their 70s, and what will millennials most need in their late 30s to mid-40s?

Here are a few examples of transitions that will create growth opportunities within industries and sectors as the massive boomer generation moves from its midlife to its retirement stage:

1. Life insurance to long-term-care insurance
2. Home renovations to home decorations
3. Ordinary vacations to cruise ships

4. Family dentistry to cosmetic and new breakthrough implants
5. Lawn and gardening equipment to "we do it for you" services
6. Weight loss to vitamins, skin care, and antiaging
7. Vacation/retirement homes to assisted-living/ nursing homes

The younger millennial generation aspires to be entrepreneurial and control their destiny even more than the baby boomers did. But there will be a substantial sector of aging boomers who will want to develop their own part-time business, from their home if possible.

Hence I recommend that such aspiring entrepreneurs consider what sectors of the markets you are interested in will benefit from the predictable aging, first of the massive baby-boom generation, and second of the emerging millennial generation.

Why I Like Healthcare

Healthcare and wellness are the largest sector of aging baby-boom spending. Here is what I like about this segment.

It should be clear from the trends discussed above that health and wellness have the best and longest-term trends of any segment of our economy. Healthcare has also grown faster than any other major consumer segment, because the costs of care have gone up and as we have increasingly aged as a society. It is now 17 percent of our GDP, and it is forecast to grow to 20 percent+ by 2030.

Nonetheless, the demands on public funding are already high and will become unbearable in the decades ahead. Governments have promised health-care benefits that they have no hope of funding with the inevitable economic slowdown ahead and the accelerating aging of our society, with fewer workers to support retirees and the elderly. (I will cover this more in chapter 3.) Hence I think that the traditional healthcare sectors, supported by Medicare, Medicaid, and insurance, will be squeezed terribly by cost caps and means testing for benefits, even though they grow in volume.

By contrast, *nontraditional health and wellness sectors are funded largely voluntarily and hence more intelligently.* People spend money out of their own pockets because they value looking better, feeling better, and potentially living longer. Such sectors should continue to do much better, despite an inevitable crisis in traditional health-care funding and costs in the decades ahead.

Know Where You Can Grow

The lesson of this chapter: whatever sector your business or product or service is in, understand—through our demographic data or your own surveys of your customers—when and how much they spend money on your product or service as they age. Once you know that, you can predict which customers and which market segments will grow or wane for years and decades in the future and where you should focus for the greatest growth and profits.

In chapter 3, I will add another simple principle to the more ominous economic trends ahead: We have seen the greatest debt and financial bubble in modern history. It can only end badly, despite endless government attempts to put a Band-Aid on it with unprecedented money printing and stimuli. In late 2018, global bubbles already started to crack. I expect one last bubble, led by the U.S. and its tax cuts; then we get a global bubble burst and a great deleveraging of debt starting most likely in 2020, or as late as 2021, if Trump can keep this bubble going an extra year to get reelected. But that will be a challenge, with my greatest cycles converging and debt growing more ominous everywhere.

Smaller companies and nimble entrepreneurs can best take advantage of the avalanche of opportunities that will prevail when larger companies fail or leave slowing market sectors. Cash and cash flow will be key to the decade ahead, in which we will see the greatest deleveraging of debt since the 1930s. It won't be pretty, and it will be anything but painless.

That's why the decade ahead will be the Entrepreneurial Decade.

Chapter Three

The Greatest Debt and Financial Bubble in Modern History

Why It Will Burst and How You Can Prosper!

I t's one thing to be able to project when demographic trends will peak in any major country or consumer sector. That is more of a science.

The hardest thing to predict is *when* a bubble is going to burst. In fact, when major bubbles like the current one occur, people go into denial; they don't want the easy gains to stop. Mostly you will hear in the media why this is *not* a bubble—why it is different this time.

Bubbles are like drugs. It's painful to come down after getting high, so people keep taking more until they hit bottom and have to go into detox.

A great example comes from dropping grains of sand to form a growing mound. As you keep dropping one after the next, the mound gets steeper. But there is a point where one grain of sand will cause a massive avalanche. That's how bubbles work! You can tell when the mound is looking shaky, but you can't predict which grain of sand will cause the avalanche. It's like the proverbial straw that breaks the camel's back.

Hence it is more of an art to predict when bubbles are likely to burst. And there is nothing more difficult than predicting that a bubble will burst when it is still going. People just don't want to hear it.

But let me tell you one thing that is crystal clear from my long-term economic research: *this is the greatest and most global debt and financial bubble in modern history.* When it finally bursts, you will need to be as safe and liquid as possible in your investments, and you will need maximum entrepreneurial creativity and flexibility to create cash and cash flow to survive and prosper. And this bubble is going to burst sooner rather than later.

I am going to start here with the ten principles of bubbles, which I cover in my most recent book, *Zero Hour.* Then I will give you some examples throughout history and show how similar they look. I will examine what causes bubbles and why we are in one, no matter how many respected experts say otherwise. These principles come from studying every major financial bubble since the mid-1600s. These principles are very consistent over time and apply to the present bubble:

1. All growth and evolution are exponential, not linear.
2. All growth is cyclical, not incremental.
3. Bubbles always burst; there are no exceptions.
4. The greater the bubble, the greater the burst.
5. Bubbles tend to go back to where they started or a bit lower.
6. Financial bubbles tend to get more extreme over time, because credit availability to fuel them expands as our incomes and wealth expand.
7. Bubbles become so attractive that they eventually suck in even the skeptics.
8. No one wants the "high" to end, so we go into denial as the bubble evolves, especially in the later stages.
9. Major bubbles only occur about once in a human lifetime, so it easy to forget the lessons from the last one.
10. Bubbles may seem fruitless and destructive when they burst, but they actually serve a very essential function in the process of innovation and human progress.

To comment a little more on these principles, the human mind is simply not wired to think in terms of exponential growth. But from any vantage point—100 years, 1,000 years, 6,000 years, and as far as you go back—

history is clearly exponential in progress. We have seen more progress in our standard of living in the last 100 years than we have seen in the 1000 years before that.

We're also not wired to think in cycles. We want to get better incrementally, and better and better ... and then go to heaven. That's not the way it works down here on earth.

Here are two simple ways to explain this mind trick. If we are told that we are going to make 3 percent a year on an investment of $100,000 a year, we picture gains of $3,000 a year. But that is not what happens in reality. That $3,000 interest compounds if reinvested, and that increases the original investment and interest every year. This is an important principle of long-term investment, called *compound interest.*

This chart shows the difference between a simple or linear 3 percent growth rate (if you took and spent your 3 percent interest every year) and a compound growth

The Power of Compounding at a Constant Growth Rate

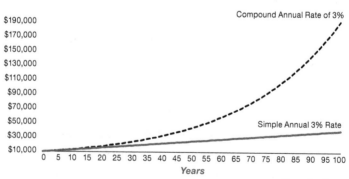

rate (if you reinvested it). Over long periods of time this makes an enormous difference. Deferral of gratification represents a huge difference between people who build long-term wealth and those who don't.

Here's another example of how the mind misinterprets reality. If you're walking down a normal road, the world clearly looks flat. But if you get in a spaceship and go up a couple hundred miles, the world is clearly round. Linear versus compound, flat versus round—these are two clear paradoxes in life and in our misperceptions.

Both of these natural misconceptions of our minds show how we often don't see the big picture or reality as it is. Understanding the exponential and cyclical nature of economic growth and progress is especially critical when we are in a once-in-a-lifetime major bubble, which comes towards the end of a long period of progress like 1945–2007.

These bubble periods are the crescendo. As I will outline in chapter 4, they are the colorful fall season before the harsh winter. Most people will not see this bubble bursting, even though we've seen a series of bubbles crash since 1987, because they don't want the party to end and they don't think exponentially and cyclically. They think that central banks and governments are more powerful than natural cycles. But whom would you bet on: God and Mother Nature, or Janet Yellen and Mario Draghi?

The first and most extreme bubble in modern history was the infamous Dutch tulip bubble, which peaked in 1637 and crashed 99 percent. That bubble was the most extreme, as it was the first for the modern world. But we were talking tulip bulbs, for crying out loud—and they went up 1,000 times in value, mostly in a year. This bubble demonstrated how human nature and greed play into the process and how bubbles always crash, regardless of why they build.

Let me show you what the first stock bubble in history looked like. The first stock was that of the East India Trading Company in 1706. Other companies were founded for ocean voyages and the spice trade. The British and French governments used them to raise money to pay debts, and they also financed purchases of shares at advantageous rates—sound a little like central-bank and Fed policies today? Below is a chart of the South Sea Company bubble in England. There

Straight Up, Straight Down
The South Seas Company Bubble

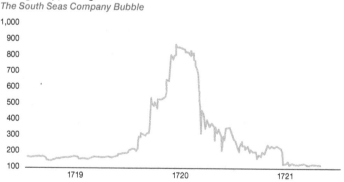

Source: "Conquer the Crash" by Robert Prechter, pg. 80; François Velde, http://www.heraldica.org/econ/

was a similar bubble in the Mississippi land bonanza in France.

This was the first period in which nonrelated investors bought shares in a company in order to finance its growth. Like with tulips, more and more people piled in. Prices got so extreme that they had to burst. That's why history shows that bubbles always burst, and the greater the bubble, the greater the burst. We ended up seeing an extreme bubble like the South Sea Company, which peaked in 1720. Sir Isaac Newton, the most respected scientist of the time, warned against that bubble, but it kept going up, until he finally got in at the end and got crushed. That's what I mean when I say that bubbles even suck in the skeptics.

There have been many major bubbles since then. There was the Midwestern and Chicago land bubble, driven by the canal revolution. That caused a massive stock and real-estate collapse in 1837, creating the greatest depression in U.S. history prior to the Great Depression. The U.S. government offered land at cheap prices and then financed those purchases at very low interest rates. That's what creates a bubble—easy speculation!

Then there was the railroad bubble, which burst from 1872 to 1877 after speculation on the first transcontinental railroads in the U.S. Then there was the Great Depression, when stocks crashed 89 percent from late 1929 to late 1932. We had bubbles in gold

Nasdaq: Two Great Bubbles, Second About to Burst

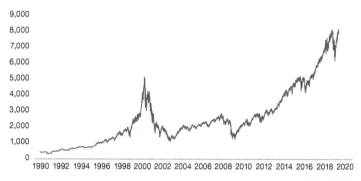

Source: Yahoo! Finance

and commodities in the inflation decade of the 1970s, which crashed in the 1980s.

Then we hit the greatest bubble of our time, greater than the Roaring Twenties bubble in stocks and farm equipment (call that a tractor bubble): the tech and Internet bubble of 1995–early 2000, shown in the chart above. As I said earlier, each bubble gets greater, as there is more income, wealth and credit to feed it.

That bubble crashed 78 percent. A second bubble is building from all of the free money being printed by governments to keep the bubble going. That's the denial principle: it's keeping the high going as it's too painful to detox and come down. But there was another bubble that followed tech stocks from 2000 to 2005: real estate.

In the Roaring Twenties, households had to put 50 percent down to buy a house, and they only got a 5-year balloon mortgage, so there wasn't much capacity to speculate. In the 1990s people could buy a house, often with no money down and no documentation of credit. Banks and investors became convinced that real estate could never go down, although history is clear that it does (denial again). In the 1930s real estate crashed 26 percent. From 2006 to 2012, it crashed 34 percent, and it has much further to go from new highs being made in 2019, as the chart below shows.

My projections demonstrate the principle that bubbles go back to where they started or a bit lower. I see a most likely scenario of a 56 percent drop from the top forming in 2019, and as much as a 67 percent worst-case drop, if they return to the lows of 1997. Countries like China have seen the greatest real-estate bubbles and could see cities like Shanghai go down as much as 78 percent!

This has not only been the greatest and most global bubble in modern history, it has been the most perva-

The Downside Risk in Second U.S. Housing Bubble
S&P/CoreLogic 10-City Home Price Index

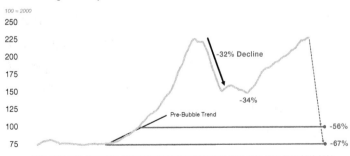

Source: Standard & Poor's Case-Shiller US 10-City Home Price Index

sive one. It has evolved into a series of bubbles—bubble after bubble—since the massive baby boom came along and exaggerated everything, and now governments are keeping the bubble going with unprecedented money printing and stimuli.

As I discussed in chapter 1, when the baby boomers was young, they created the greatest inflation in modern history (an inflation bubble) with the expense of incorporating them into the workforce before they became productive. Along with that came a boom in commodity prices and the biggest bubble in gold and silver. Those bubbles crashed starting in 1980.

Then we had the first mini-stock bubble from 1983 to1987. Stocks crashed 40 percent in a matter of weeks. Then the infamous tech bubble, the greatest real estate bubble globally ever, then the bubble in emerging country stocks—look at China's stock market (chart, next page). It went up 464 percent in just 2 years and then crashed 72 percent. In 2014, it rose 159 percent into 2015—just one year, and has crashed 49 percent into early 2016 and looks to be heading for a 72 percent+ crash into 2021 or 2022 from its projected high in late 2019 or so, back to 3600+. Then commodities peaked again in 2008 and gold in 2011. Gold has been crashing ever since and likely has much further to go.

Finally, we have what I see as the *final bubble*, as this one has been created almost totally from desperate and artificial stimuli.

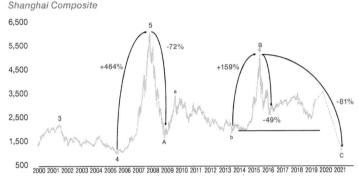

Second China Bubble Will Burst Further
Shanghai Composite

Source: Yahoo! Finance

What normally happens is that you see a convergence of demographic and technological trends, which cause abnormal investment gains. People borrow more and get overly speculative. A natural bubble builds and then bursts suddenly at some point.

Since the crash of 2008–09, the demographic trends and the rapid growth of the Internet have no longer been driving the boom and bubble. It's been unprecedented stimulus and bailouts. This money has not been lent by banks to expand capacity and jobs, as we overexpanded in the bubble boom already. It's simply gone into speculation. And that never ends well.

The gold bugs have been calling for hyperinflation from such money printing, but I have been calling for a massive bubble burst, which will lead to deflation in prices, and not just in consumer prices. It will be massive in financial assets, as in the 1930s. And indeed, despite such massive money creation and stimulus, we've seen inflation fall more than rise, staying in a 0–2 percent range. Without this unprecedented stimulus, we would have clearly had deflation in prices already. The true story is that governments are fighting 1930s-style deflation with massive inflation. Hence deflation is the underlying trend!

Here's what the gold bugs don't understand: *when you see a depression or deflation in prices throughout history, it is always preceded by a major debt and financial bubble.*

In the simplest terms, debt grows much faster than the economy and fuels a bubble in stocks and financial assets. When the final grain of sand hits and the bubble bursts, massive amounts of money disappear. How does this happen? Debts get written down, banks fail. Debt is a way of creating money. As much as 50 percent of those debts can simply be erased, and that money disappears. It's like magic: now you see it, now you don't.

Financial assets from stocks to real estate bubble up and create lots of wealth; then that disappears by 70–90 percent in just a few years. (Do you know that it took stocks 24 years—to 1953—to get back to the 1929 bubble peak?) This sudden wealth is money to people, and then it disappears! Now you see it, now you don't.

The next chart shows something obvious but which most economists totally missed. Total debt in the U.S.

(government and private) grew at 2.54 times the rate of GDP or economic growth for 25 years from 1983 to 2008. Total debt to GDP ratio in 2018 was 3.67, and it's still rising. This has happened to similar degrees in most countries around the world. That is simply not sustainable. That is a debt bubble—and along with that came all of the financial-asset bubbles I covered earlier—from stocks to real estate to emerging stocks to gold.

Any economist that does not see a financial crisis coming after such debt growth has not studied history; I don't care how many PhDs you have.

It's even worse than this chart shows. There is another sector of debt that is unique to our lifetimes: unfunded entitlements for Medicaid, Medicare, and Social Security. The most conservative independent estimates of the amount of future promises that don't have funding to back them is *$70 trillion*. That's almost as much as all normal private and government debt

U.S. Debt-Fueled Bubble Boom Hasn't Deleveraged
U.S. Debt vs. GDP Growth

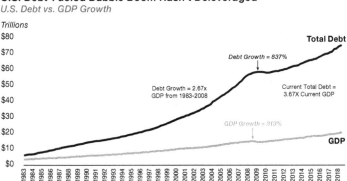

Source: St. Louis Federal Reserve, Treasury Direct

combined. And it will only grow when a bad economy reduces the contributions and increases the payouts.

These unfunded entitlement obligations are high in most countries and even higher in many European countries, with faster-aging populations. Everyone wanted to die and go to heaven. That is not going to happen here on earth.

The truth is that total U.S. debt in 2014 is: $26.8 trillion government + $45.9 trillion private + $4 trillion foreign + $70 trillion (est.) unfunded entitlements = $146.7 trillion. That's over 7 times GDP.

Just for comparison, the total debt to GDP ratio in 1929 at the top of the last great debt bubble was 1.9 times GDP, back when we didn't have unfunded entitlements!

At the peak of the bubble in 2008, the private debt hit $42 trillion versus $10 trillion for federal debt. Which is the 800-pound gorilla? Of that private debt, $21 trillion came just between 2000 and 2008. History suggests that bubble will erase itself, and $20 trillion plus of debt will be restructured or fail altogether and disappear.

The net worth of households in the U.S. has expanded to new highs of $81 trillion after falling steeply in 2008–09. Last time around, that fell $16 trillion before the government printed money rapidly to stop the meltdown. Next time I see at least $25 trillion+ disappearing.

Between debt restructuring and financial assets crashing, in the years ahead we could see $45 trillion+ in money disappear in the U.S. alone. That's more like $120 trillion+ globally. That is the textbook definition of deflation: fewer dollars chasing the same goods. Hence prices fall.

We've seen inflation all of our lives. That has had a lot to do with the massive baby boom hitting the scene, that pig moving through a python. Between 2015 and 2020+ we will see deflation. We actually saw deflation briefly between late 2008 and early 2009, before governments started printing money at the speed of light to offset it. Does suppressing a symptom lead to better health?

So this debt and financial speculation bubble started to burst in 2008, but governments decided to print more money than was being destroyed to stop it. You can't do that forever. You can't keep a drug habit going forever, and you can't keep a bubble going forever. Financial detox is inevitable at some point—when that final pebble of sand hits the mound and causes an avalanche.

If we look back at history, we can see the three greatest debt bubbles since 1870 (using the U.S. again as an example of what has happened around the world). Note that the greatest bubble and depression to follow before this data peaked in 1835 and crashed into 1843. That bubble in the U.S. was created by the expansion into the Midwest, when the government was giving people cheap land and low-interest financing. That is the perfect stage for a bubble, like the first stock bubble, which peaked in 1720, with speculation financed by governments.

You can see in the chart below how each debt bubble gets greater, as there is greater income and credit to fuel it. After the first debt-ratio peak in the early 1870s, we saw that railroad depression I described from 1873 to 1877. Debt ratios came back down. But since that was not as great a debt or financial speculation bubble, neither the depression nor the debt write-offs were as deep.

Then you see the Great Depression, which followed the Roaring Twenties bubble and higher debt ratios. Do you realize that towards the end of that bubble, 40 percent of all bank loans were going to finance stock speculation? How could that end well?

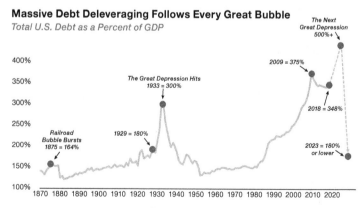

Massive Debt Deleveraging Follows Every Great Bubble
Total U.S. Debt as a Percent of GDP

Source: Courtesy of Hoisington Investment Management, Dent Research

But a lot of people don't realize that that was a tractor bubble in farming as well. Henry Ford's new assembly line shot autos in urban areas from 10 percent to 90 percent of households from 1914 to 1929. But it also created a massive productivity revolution in farms through tractors. We were still mostly farmers back then, and people borrowed against their farmland and equipment. When that bubble burst, it was the smaller banks lending to local farmers that tended to be crushed, as opposed to the larger multinational banks, which are creating low-cost mortgages for consumers and mortgage securities for unsuspecting investors today.

Look at how much higher debt got in the U.S. in the recent bubble—over twice that as a percent of GDP in 1929. The greater the bubble, the greater the burst. If we look around the world, we can see that total debt ratios mostly range from 300 percent of GDP to 500 percent, with a few outliers on each side.

Total Debt to GDP Ratios Around the World

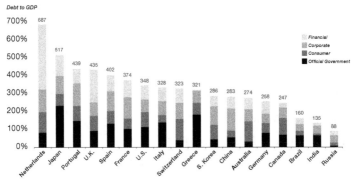

Source: "Debt and (Not Much) Deleveraging," McKinsey Global Institute, February 2015

The countries with the highest debt ratios are the Netherlands, at 687 percent; Japan, at 517 percent; Portugal, at 439 percent; the U.K., at 435 percent; and Spain; at 402 percent. Countries in the middle range from France, at 374 percent, to Greece, at 320 percent They include Italy, Switzerland, and the U.S. in between. On the lower side of the developed world, at just under 300 percent, are South Korea, Germany, Canada, and Australia.

China is off the charts for emerging countries, which can't bear as much debt because of lower incomes and creditworthiness. It is at 283 percent versus Brazil, which at 160 percent; India, at 135 percent; and Russia at a mere 88 percent. Make no mistake about it: from every major measure, this is the greatest and most global debt and financial bubble ever. Deflation and depression have to be on the other side.

Let's return to the simplest logic about debt and bubbles.

Debt is not *like* a drug. It *is* a performance-enhancing financial drug. Like any drug, from sugar to coffee to alcohol to cocaine to pain pills to heroin, which make you feel better or perform better today, this comes at the expense of the future. None of these things are known for making you healthier, only unhealthier. You are borrowing from the future.

It's the same with debt and speculation. Debt allows you to buy more with your same income today, but at the expense of tomorrow. You will have less spending power in the future, because you will paying back the debt and, in many cases, even more in interest.

That does not mean that it doesn't make sense to get a normal 30-year mortgage to finance a house that you need while your kids are growing up (not later, when you don't need it) or to finance a car over 5 years, the period you plan to use it. But when people borrow to purchase more than that or to speculate, it always increases your standard of living today at the expense of tomorrow. That's why debt and financial-asset bubbles are not sustainable and always burst.

The next chart is my favorite for showing that debt is *exactly* like a drug. It takes more and more to create less and less effect until the side effects of the drug drain your health or kill you. Since the 1960s, for each extra dollar of debt, we have clearly gotten less and less growth in GDP, as this chart below shows. We hit the

Diminishing Returns in Debt: Nearing Zero Point
Gain in GDP per Dollar of Debt Added

Source: Dent Research, St. Louis Federal Reserve

zero point in 2009. Then QE and money printing gave us a quick reprieve, whose impact is retreating fast. There is a point where taking more of a drug doesn't work any longer.

The people who work in the wellness arena will understand the principle of detox. When you get too toxic from stimulants and bad foods, the only good choice is to go through detox first, get the bad stuff that keeps you addicted out of your system, and then get on a healthier diet.

I heard a health expert say that "pain is bad stuff leaving the body." That's why people don't want to go through health or financial detox. But the smart people who do know the benefits embrace it and appreciate the pain. It is actually a sign you are getting healthier!

Our global economy is getting ready to go through a deep detox, or depression, with deflation in prices and high failure rates in jobs, businesses, and banks. Most people will not see this coming, because of their bubble highs and delusions. But you can see it coming and position yourself to become more entrepreneurial and more defensive in your investments. You can not only survive but prosper in a period like this. I see this "winter" season ahead as the most opportune period for entrepreneurs.

In chapter 4, I will look at why the period up to 2022 or so is the most likely time for such a depression and entrepreneurial explosion, like the 1930s, and why this crisis could last longer in many countries. Some countries will never fully recover, as their demographic trends only get worse for decades to come. Emerging countries like India will lead the next global boom.

I will show my ultimate cycle: the 80-Year Four-Season Economic Cycle, and the four primary cycles that drive it, including, but beyond, demographics.

Chapter Four

The Four-Season Economic Model and the Four Primary Cycles Driving It
Why You Have to Have Different Strategies for Each Season

I n prehistoric times, we figured out how to predict the four seasons annually. That was a big part of the agricultural revolution, which was the last big bang in economic history before the Industrial Revolution in the late 1700s.

The history of mankind has shown our ability to increasingly understand our world and to predict more processes—weather, physics, biology—so that we can better plan ahead and automate more tasks in order to free ourselves for higher and more profitable things.

Human beings are the only species that have the brain power to see the future, including our death, which makes us a bit more neurotic. But this capacity also makes us far more prosperous. Hence it's natural that this process would continue. Why wouldn't we be able to predict our economy and its natural seasons decades in advance—even beyond the boom-and-bust cycles I presented in chapter 1?

If you see the bigger picture and understand that our economy evolves in four seasons or stages, you can see the "flavor" and changing dynamics of the economy, not just the booms and busts. The spring boom is very different from the fall boom, just as the summer bust is very different from the winter bust. Each of these four seasons rewards different personal, business, and investment strategies.

At Harvard Business School, the biggest single insight I got was something called the *product life cycle*. This has four clear stages: *innovation*, *growth*, *shakeout*, and *maturity*. *Invention* before innovation and *decline* after maturity are two other natural phases, but these overlap with the cycles before and to follow. In the maturity phase, the next invention phase occurs; in the decline stage, the next innovation stage occurs and so on. This four-stage cycle occurs at all levels including technologies, industries, nations, empires, and so on.

Most businesses get in trouble because they keep doing what made them successful in the previous stage or season; then things change, and they start to fail. The entrepreneur who was a great innovator and disruptor fails when the product finally catches on and moves mainstream. It now needs systems for growth and expansion of distribution into broader markets. Once they are fully mainstream and their market matures, dominant companies have new entrepreneurial products and companies chipping away at them from all angles. Like elephants, they have no way to compete against such nimble challengers.

The same goes for investors. The investments that did well in the inflationary 1970s were very different from the ones that did well in the bubble boom of the 1980s forward. Now we are headed into a new normal of very slow growth or decline and deflation in prices, like the 1930s—something that almost none of us have seen in our lifetimes. That alone explains why gold, commodities, and real estate did so well in the last prolonged financial downturn of the 1970s but will tank beyond anyone's expectations in the economic downturn of the years ahead.

The life cycles of everything I have studied—from weather to human life to products and industries to nations and empires—grows and evolves in four stages or "seasons." In modern times, our economy grows in an 80-year, two-generation, four-season life cycle. This insight adds a new dimension to economics that economists largely don't understand.

Just as we have spring, summer, fall, and winter in our annual seasons, we have youth, adulthood, midlife, and retirement in our human life cycles. Why would this not be the case for our economic cycles. It is, and very clearly! In other words:

Our economy grows in the same life cycles as we do as human beings.

The S-Curve

Before I get to this big-picture cycle, I want to introduce another simple but powerful concept: the S-curve. I first discovered this in 1979 at Bain and Company on a consulting assignment to Firestone Tire Company.

At that time, with rising oil prices and bias tires being replaced by radials (which last over twice as long), it was clear that Firestone was being too optimistic. Since I had the strongest financial background on the team, I was assigned to develop a new model for tire demand. This is when I first learned how to make a long-term forecast and discovered the power of simple, fundamental indicators versus complex models.

I developed a simple two-variable model that forecast past demand as well as Firestone's very complex model but diverged greatly from it in the future. The key component was forecasting the rise of radial tires versus bias on an S-curve. This had already happened with Michelin in France, so I could see the S-curve in action.

I quickly realized that this was a universal principle of growth and progress. I discovered the S-curve and the four-stage product life cycle before demographics. But like demographics, this is a universal cycle that works from the most micro levels to the most macro. Most economic courses see the micro and macro levels as very different—glad I didn't keep taking those courses!

To make this idea simple, it takes the same time to go from commercialization to 10 percent adoption by the consumers or businesses that are your potential market as it takes to go from 10 percent to 90 percent. That means you make 9 times the progress in the same time after the product or technology hits the tipping point at 10 percent and rapidly moves mainstream after having proven itself in more affluent and/or sophisticated niche markets. You can see how important it is for a business not to miss this acceleration—but most do and let someone else race past them.

S-Curve of Urban Automobile Consumer Adoption

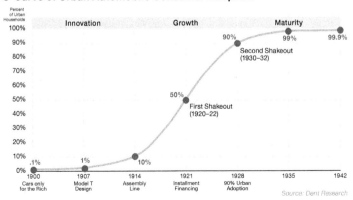

Source: Dent Research

In the U.S. at that time it had taken 7 years for radial tires to get 10 percent of the car market. My model projected that that would go to 90 percent in the next 7 years, and that is what happened. Given that radial tires lasted over twice as long, this changed the forecast for the type (radial) and cut the forecasts for the level of production capacity Firestone would need in the years ahead. We had them shut down bias-tire plants and convert to or build one that made radials. This was a massive shift in strategy.

This may be the only reason Firestone exists today. But it was already too late by the time we came in. Michelin and Bridgestone had already passed them. They understood the S-curve long before Firestone and Goodyear in the U.S., so the latter two never caught up with them.

One of the first great documentations of the S-curve came with automobiles in the early 1900s. Because of the Model T innovation by Ford, autos penetrated 10 percent of urban households from 1900 to 1914. The market was urban, as the rural areas still did not have the roads and service stations to accommodate autos. From 1914 to 1928 autos went predictably from 10 percent to 90 percent. But that was only in the more affluent urban markets, which back then were at most 50 percent of the country.

But there's another important point. Every S-curve breaks down into two overlapping S-curves within it.

And every S-curve becomes a part of a larger, two-S-curve cycle beyond it. When each S-curve is progressing in the dynamic 10 percent to 90 percent growth surge, you have the strongest boom. When one S-curve is maturing (90 percent to 99 percent) and the next is only emerging into niche markets (1 percent to 10 percent), growth stagnates. Look at the chart below.

If I looked at the broader auto industry's emergence from 1900 into 1965 into all households, I would see four stages, as in the chart: innovation from 1900 to 1914 (0.1 percent to 10 percent of first S-curve of urban adoption); growth from 1914 to 1929 (10 percent to 90 percent growth surge); shakeout from 1930 to 1945 (overlap of urban and rural; the Great Depression and World War II) and after that, a maturity boom (10 percent to 90 percent rural adoption) into the 1960s. By 1965, 80 percent of all households had at least one car, and the federal interstate highway system had been almost fully built.

Overlapping S-Curves Within Four-Season Business Cycle
Four Season Cycle

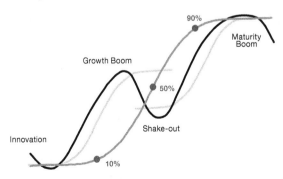

In the maturity phase of one major industry S-curve, a new iteration rises. We can see this with computers. The trend started with the first ENIAC in 1946, which came out of an innovation stage in the 1930s and 1940s. There was a growth boom in mainframes into 1965, a shakeout with minicomputers into 1984, and a maturity boom with PCs, the Internet, and cell phones into 2007–10.

This S-curve, with overlapping S-curve cycles, occurs in all product, technology, and industry life cycles. You as an entrepreneur or business owner or manager need to understand where your business is in this S-curve progression and the broader four-season cycle of innovation, growth boom, shakeout, and maturity boom over a broader time period. Those cycles can be very different for different products or industries.

The Four Seasons

To return to my previous point: our economy has a four-season economic cycle. In modern times, it progresses over two generations of innovation followed by spending booms and busts, and a seasonal cycle of inflation that progresses just like temperature in our annual weather cycles—from spring to summer (high inflation) to fall to winter (deflation).

Think of rising inflation as rising temperatures in spring that peak in late summer, and falling inflation or deflation like cooling temperatures in fall that get very cold into late winter. That is the inflation line in the chart below. And recall from chapter 1 that we can project inflation trends decades ahead, because they correlate most with workforce growth. This in turn is largely driven demographically, by the predictable entry of new workers and the retirement of older workers.

The second line is the boom-and-bust cycle of each generation, with two booms and two busts, which correspond to the four seasons. These cycles are even more predictable than the inflation cycles, because we can lag the immigration-adjusted birth index forward to find each generation's spending peak.

The Bob Hope generation had a boom from 1943 to 1968 on a 44-year lag. That occurred in the spring season with mildly rising inflation (after a deflationary winter season from 1930 to 1942). Then a bust from 1969 through 1982 during the high and peaking inflation or

Big Picture: 80-Year Four-Season Economic Cycle
The Worst of Winter is Still Ahead

summer season. They called that season "stagflation," as we saw rising inflation and worsening recessions. Economists did not know what to make of that back then and still don't know what actually caused it— boomers entering the workforce at great expense and low productivity at first.

Then came the massive baby boom and all of the immigrants. On a 46-year lag we saw the greatest boom in history from 1983 to 2007 in the fall season, with falling inflation. This means lower interest rates, which means lower mortgage costs and greater speculation in investments, among other things. The fall season is always the most dynamic, with the greatest demographic growth, falling interest rates, and new technologies moving mainstream and dramatically increasing productivity. This is where you always see bubbles in debt and financial assets. The last fall bubble boom peaked in 1929 after the explosion of the Roaring Twenties.

The winter season started in 2008, as baby-boom spending was due to fall from 2008 into 2022–23. Prices plummet in the winter season, and we get the first deflationary trends since the 1930s. The winter season brings the economy back down to earth after the glorious fall, with blazing colors and the peaking of a long trend in technologies (like computers) dating back to the last winter season moving into spring. Excess debt is deleveraged and wrung out of the economy (and as I showed in chapter 3, oh, what a debt bubble we had!). Banks fail or are taken over by stronger banks as their loan portfolios and investments are decimated. Speculation is beaten out of stocks and real estate and everything else. Investors who keep listening to their stockbrokers get slaughtered as everything goes down and asset allocation and diversification fail to work. Businesses that do not dominate their markets and/or are not efficient go out of business, or they are bought or taken over by stronger companies.

This is a survival-of-the-fittest shakeout period. It makes the whole economy sounder, more affordable, and more efficient so it can grow again after a dynamic fall bubble boom that catapults new technologies and industries into the mainstream into a peak of the whole 80-year cycle. The winter shifts market share to the strong and flushes out the weak. This is a *Great Reset*. It prepares fertile ground for growth again and for the next spring season, which ushers in a whole new era of technologies and a new set of generations. And recall that in this winter season the worst will come in the final crash and downturn, which should be more like 1930–32. Why? We took the easy way out through printing $16 trillion+ in money globally through central banks to kick the can down the road.

The winter season is like a huge financial detox after a strong and excessive period of growth and innovation. Deflation is the detox agent. When prices fall, less efficient companies cannot make profits and are flushed out. When financial assets fall, the aging generation loses money, but this makes real estate and stocks more affordable for investing for the next generation coming along. Banks go under when things like real estate fall and they have to write off or down their loans.

Why would the broader economy not favor the emerging new generation rather than the dying older generation? This is what nature does.

Conversely, this debt detox takes a great burden off consumers and businesses. It enhances their future cash flow at the expense of failing banks and bondholders, who lose money. When prices go down, the cost of living becomes more attractive for the rising generation. Unemployment goes to extremes (like 25 percent in the Great Depression). This forces many workers to look to new emerging companies and industries to find jobs and leave the old ones forever. People and companies are the most motivated and innovative in crises, not in good times. Hence this is the most accelerated period of change and opportunity.

The winter season is the most challenging and most rewarding of the four seasons for those who see it coming, especially for those that are more entrepreneurial and fast to respond. The winter season forces the economy to change more rapidly and to shift to the next dynamic growth industries, jobs, S-curves, and the needs of the next rising generation. It is a great and necessary reset. If you see this reset coming, the world is your oyster. If you don't, you will get beaten to death until you figure out that you have to change and find a way to get in sync with the next 80-year cycle.

Of course, all this change and creative destruction creates a gaping hole for the most innovative businesses and for new entrepreneurial opportunities. When companies fail, there are opportunities for entrepreneurs to create new business models and take over certain market segments. They can do business differently and start with little or no debt or past overheads, entitlements, or entanglements.

Ultimately, cash and cash flow are the key to the winter season. Financial assets are on sale; new business opportunities suddenly open up. But only the people and companies that have cash and cash flow can take advantage of it, as neither banks nor investors will be there to support you. I see the coming period as the greatest sale on financial assets of a lifetime. I see it as a time for businesses to leap past their competitors when they are struggling and overwhelmed by the change and challenges.

The combination of the demographic slowdown and the financial detox (debt and bubble burst) of this winter season will create a vast pool of dislocated workers and salespeople, who will be looking for a way to survive and prosper again. *This should be the opportunity of a lifetime for prospecting in an industry like network marketing*, if you see it coming and acquire the skills and join the right company to take advantage of it.

The more entrepreneurial, aggressive, and creative you are, the more you and/or your business will succeed. The strongest companies in every industry or sector will be challenged, but they will grow stronger and will have less competition in the spring boom and 80-year cycle to follow.

If you're looking now for a better company to work for, find one that will survive because they dominate their markets and/or are the lowest cost or highest quality. Will Apple and Samsung survive in the consumer computing space? You bet they will—but many more also-rans will not. The same goes for networking marketing. In the products that most interest you, find the companies that have the strongest products, the best training and marketing support, and the largest market shares.

This is also the time when new companies with superior products and or business models will emerge out of the ashes. That means companies that are finding new market niches that failing companies are leaving or that that are just emerging and haven't been recognized yet. You can be such an entrepreneur in your markets, or you can join a company that fits that bill.

You don't want to be in a mediocre, middle-of-the-road company or business. Either be with one of the dominant companies that survive and rapidly gain market share from failing competitors, or be with a new, emerging company that has an edge, is growing fast, and benefits from the opportunities that open up from economic breakdown.

Although the four seasons are different in many ways, the common denominators are that stocks do well in the booms and poorly in the busts. They do the best in the fall bubble boom and the worst in the winter deflation season.

Entrepreneurs do the best in the off seasons: the summer and winter busts. When times get tough, entrepreneurs go shopping. In the inflationary summer season, the next killer apps in all industries emerge. These will suddenly go mainstream on an S-curve in the fall bubble boom. The killer apps for computers were not the original mainframes, but the PC and cell phones that emerged in the late 1970s. Most of the growth companies in the last boom from 1983 to 2007 were start-ups in the inflationary summer season from 1969 to 1982. Computer chips, personal computers, cell phones, timeshare computing (the beginning of the Internet), Apple, Microsoft, Dell, Walmart, Home Depot, Charles Schwab, and many other new products and companies emerged into niche markets and then went mainstream at the speed of light in the fall boom to follow.

In the broader computer cycle, mainframes emerged in the spring season, then minicomputers in the summer season and then PCs and the Internet in the fall season. Now that we are already well into the winter season since 2008, what do we see? Social media. This is the maturing phase of computers and makes them much more human. But the winter season will see a whole array of totally new technologies emerge: biotech, robotics, 3D printer manufacturing, nano-technologies, breakthroughs in alternative energy. and things we don't even see yet. These technologies will drive the next 80-year cycle.

In chapter 5, I will discuss the new direct-marketing and network revolutions that are creating the best entrepreneurial options for the next decade and beyond. Note that *network marketing* has two of the key words in its name.

The Four Primary Cycles Driving Our Economy beyond Demographics

My innovations in economics started in the 1980s with the S-curve and product life cycle, demographics and the consumer life cycle, and this 80-year four-season model. Those innovations had all come together by 1989, in my first book, *Our Power to Predict*.

Those innovations were enough for me to see major trends that almost no one saw for the 1990s: the great-est boom and stock-market bubble in history; the fall of Japan (which looked like China today); falling inflation;

an S-curve of technological acceleration from the mid-1990s forward; and a great real-estate boom. But the early 2000s brought some new twists, which forced me to dig deeper, as did the unprecedented stimulus from central banks around the world that came later in the decade.

History clearly shows that cycles do repeat, but it's more that they rhyme, as there are always new twists from technological and human progress. These new twists led me to three other primary cycles. These give a more complete picture of this 80-year four-season economic cycle and help us better see the key turning points. I summarize these four primary cycles in the chart below, starting with the Generational Spending Wave I covered in depth in chapter 1.

The demographic cycle on top is still the most fundamental and the most projectable, making it still my greatest breakthrough. And it is even better given that

Hierarchy of Macroeconomic Cycles: Worst Ahead 2020–2022
Developed Countries

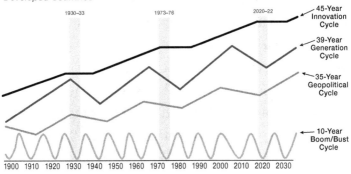

Source: Dent Research

we can project the microcycles of most pertinent consumer sectors. If I just told you that the economy was going to be the worst in your lifetime and that would be good for prospecting, you wouldn't be nearly as excited as if I told you that most of your industry was going to see the strongest years of spending in the decades ahead.

The generational or demographic waves have peaked every 39 years in the last century: in 1929, 1968, and 2007 for the stock market and the broader economy. How's that for a time cycle? The next down cycle bottoms between around 2020 and 2023 before turning up again in the longer term. But it's a good thing I have the direct means to project such cycles as the millennial generation. This will drive the next boom, and it is composed of 2 major waves. It won't peak 39 years from now, but on either side of that. The first will peak around 2036–37, the second around 2056.

The next cycle, which I discovered in late 2005, is called the geopolitical cycle. This cycle is positive for about 18 years and then turns negative. I tracked this back 200 years, and it was typically 16–19 years—another clear cycle. In recent times, we saw a positive geopolitical cycle, where almost nothing went wrong in the world from 1983 to 2000—18 years. Then the tech crash got violent in 2001, and the next thing you knew we saw the geopolitical event of our times: 9/11.

Since then there has been one challenging event after the next: the ill-fated Iraq war; the Afghanistan war; the Arab Spring and revolts across Egypt, Libya, and Tunisia; Somalian pirates; the brutal Syrian civil war; the rise of ISIS; and most recently the Russian push into the Crimea and Ukraine.

The global geopolitical environment will only tend to get worse until around late 2019 or early 2020. Then this cycle turns positive again from 2020 to 2036. All of a sudden, the world will start to get more stable and peaceful again, and no one will know why. You will!

The most recent primary cycle I added was an innovation cycle, which peaks around every 45 years. It is the most important in the longer term, especially in the artificially created bubble of 2009–19. The Industrial Revolution of the late 1700s greatly elevated the importance of this cycle, as did the emergence of the first middle class after World War II for the Generational Spending Wave.

In the past, I tried to tie innovation cycles to the generation cycle. Although there is a good correlation, it never quite clicked. From my historical economic and technology research I finally saw that there were very clear watersheds in major technologies right at every 45 years: The factory revolution in 1830; steamships and canals in 1875; railroads and telegraphs in 1920; autos, electricity, phones, radios and TVs in 1965; and personal computers and the Internet around 2010. This broad cycle increases the general productivity of workers and companies. It occurs when the technologies are moving mainstream—not when they are invented or moving only into niche markets. The great surge in railroads was from 1897 to 1920. One of the clearest peaks came in 1920, when railroad passenger traffic and revenue peaked. After that, it fell off consistently as cars, trucks, and buses were on the rise.

As I mentioned earlier, there was a clear surge in auto adoption and the creation of highway systems from 1947 to 1965, which reached its peak in 1964–65: 18 years again. Since 2010–12, everyone has been on the Internet through some device. Now it's just about how to make them faster and better and to do more perverted things on them for fun and social impact. The main impact on business and productivity is over.

This 45-year innovation cycle peaked around 2010 and turns down into 2032 before turning up again into 2055. Unlike the geopolitical cycle, this cycle doesn't have a negative effect when it turns down. It's more that the productivity dividends from rapid innovation stall or flatten out.

But this cycle also sees a hype bubble for the next early-stage technologies ahead. This is very exaggerated at first and extends the stock market run for up to 9 years. The current hype phase is over social media and cryptocurrencies, etc. The bubble from that is not due to peak until around late 2019. Hence of the larger three cycles in the chart, this will be the last to peak and turn down. Historically, every other cycle causes the greatest bubbles and resets/depressions to follow every 90 years. See chart below.

The present hype cycle seems to be peaking around late 2019 or early 2020—right near the 90-year anniversary of the greatest bubble top in modern history, in late 1929! That makes this double-45, or 90-year cycle the most important one in this time period. It is calling for a major depression and financial-asset and stock bubble burst, most likely between 2020 and 2023.

This great reset will light up the Entrepreneurial Decade ahead. It will cause a great shakeout in business and banking and create whole new opportunities for new solutions from the micro to the macro level. Newer firms, small and large, who think differently and come up with radical new solutions will prosper the most.

Finally, there is the most effective shorter-term cycle I have discovered since the Generational Spend-

90-Year Great Resets Since Industrial Revolution
Stock Prices Since 1700

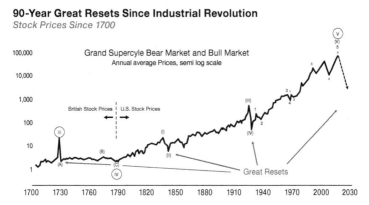

Source: Conquer the Crash by Robert Prechter, pg. 33, Dent Research

ing Wave hit in 2013. I had been using a 10-year boom-bust cycle from analyst Ned Davis that saw the worst stock crashes and recessions in the first 2–3 years of every new decade. It worked like a charm until 2010–12, when I first expected the next great crash to follow the 2008–09 crash—and that crash came earlier than usual on this cycle.

Through one of the top fund managers in the U.S., I found a solar cycle, which affects radiation, rainfall, and many other things and which correlates better. It is pretty accurately tracked and projected by top scientists at NASA and Stanford University. This cycle varies between 8 and 14 years, with an average of 10 years.

Now here's why this cycle is so powerful. I went back to the mid-1800s, where there is good data on stocks, recessions, and financial crises, and I found that 88 percent of such crashes and crises occurred in the downward part of this cycle.

The last boom/bust cycle peaked in early 2000 right at the top of the NASDAQ and tech bubble. The bottom of that cycle hit right at the bottom of the Great Recession in mid-2009. The most recent cycle peaked later than usual in early 2014 and at this time is projected to bottom around late 2020; it could come a bit later.

This 10-year boom/bust cycle, along with our other three longer-term ones, means that the next great crash is highly likely to hit first between late 2019 and late 2020, with the weakest broader period being 2020–

23. That's when we should see the worst of the winter or depression season before the next global spring boom from 2023 to 2036–37.

Most importantly, the only time that all four of these primary cycles have been down at the same time were 1930–34 and 1969–76. Those were clearly the worst stock crashes and financial crises of the last century. After late 2019—look out again.

After honing into these four cycles over the last thirty-five years of my research, I will say this: if we don't see a major stock crash and economic crisis start by late 2021, I will quit my profession and become a limo driver in Australia! That's how confident I am.

My strong warning to you is that I see the worst economic downturn of your lifetime coming as we move into early 2020 and possibly a few years beyond that. This is the time to become an entrepreneur in any way possible. This is a time to wake up and get more serious about your life, your business, your family, and your investments.

This is a time of deflation, when cash and cash flow will be the most important financial assets. How do you do anything to increase these? What assets can you sell? Where can you make extra money? How do you become your own business in the best sectors so as to shield yourself from the inevitable job shock ahead?

In chapter 5, I will look at the direct-marketing and network revolutions that are changing our economy in this broader information revolution.

Chapter Five

The Direct-Marketing and Network Revolution

Four New Marketing Models and How Network Marketing Fits In

Every new 80-year economic cycle brings a new revolution in technologies and in business models and in how we live and work.

The last revolution brought standardized products like the Model T (1907) and the assembly line (1914) from Ford. It also introduced a new, more decentralized corporate model, which took decisions and strategies more down to the product levels at corporations like General Motors, through the genius of Alfred Sloan (1921). This new organizational model gave the greatest long-term benefits by redesigning how we manage, work, and communicate. That's how General Motors beat Ford from the early 1930s forward in the winter shakeout season, which ultimately determines what companies succeed in the longer term.

The early 1900s brought a mass-production revolution in manufacturing and a more decentralized model for top-down management to replace the top-down bureaucratic organization of the previous era, as modeled by the railroads and Great Britain.

Over the last few decades and into many decades ahead, we are seeing two revolutions:

1. A direct-marketing revolution, which cuts layers of distribution and bureaucracy, ultimately with more responsive, customized products and personalized service.

2. A network mode of organization that is not only more decentralized but is customer-centric, operating from the bottom up, not from the top down.

More people will become their own business, either on their own or within larger companies. They will be rewarded for their results and contribution to profits, not merely on a salary basis (with raises at best if you do well). There will also be less job security in a more uncertain world.

Welcome to the new network economy. This is a revolution, and it is already coming from the most entrepreneurial companies, like Apple, Google, Facebook, and Alibaba, and even from financial-planning firms like Edward Jones, as well as from eBay, Amazon, Tupperware, and network-marketing firms. They offer more direct marketing and a bottoms-up, more entrepreneurial model. But this revolution will come even more from entrepreneurs and the most entrepreneurial smaller companies in the decades ahead.

Why do I tell you about this macrotrend? Because the new economy is ultimately about making more and more people entrepreneurs, even within larger companies (although that's the last place it will manifest fully). But the next decade, with its major economic challenges, will most favor people who find a way to turn what they naturally do—for their companies, for their friends—into THEIR own business. If you can do that by networking with a larger company or information infrastructure, your odds of success and rewards will only be greater.

When we look back in history, we will see the coming decade as the Entrepreneurial Decade, much like the 1930s and 1970s. *This is the time to become your own business.* You don't have to wait and look back at history and wish you had been part of it. You can see the future now and position yourself to prosper in the worst decade of our lifetimes, which is just ahead.

The Internet and its many platforms, from eBay to Amazon to Alibaba, have already made it much easier for everyday people to start their own businesses through a broad and efficient online infrastructure. Social media adds a whole new dimension on the more human scale. These info-infrastructures also make it easier to for you to expand a network-marketing business, if you choose to do so.

You can now create your own business out of your own home or small office, and you have the backing for finance, branding, marketing support, and training from a larger company—but you are still your own business and are rewarded for your entrepreneurial efforts. Network-marketing and franchise companies are the best examples of that.

You can start your own business through your personal contacts, or on the Internet or through social media. You can build a business step-by-step. You don't have to leave your present job or business until you prove you can make it on your own.

Another great approach is to find a product or service you love and connect with other people locally. Then if you prove it locally, you expand through the Internet and make it a national success.

Larger companies will have front-line sales and service people who know everything about their customers and can custom-design products and services to their needs in real time, with little or no bureaucracy. And they can provide real, personalized service, not like that of the impersonal computer-generated models (which are OK for very standardized products).

Imagine that you or your small team in that company are your own business and are accountable for your results and get direct feedback from your customers and are rewarded on the profits you create, like a small business or entrepreneur.

Imagine that you create a new product or service. The larger organization spins you off into a new venture, providing start-up financing and distribution capacities to expand if you prove your concept.

Imagine being able to work from your home part-time or full-time. Imagine doing what you do best without having a boss or supervisor second-guess everything you do and having the politics of that relationship, or of your company, dictate your future.

Or imagine leaving your company and subcontracting what you used to do for them part-time from your home, and then marketing similar services to other companies. That's a win-win for you, the entrepreneur, and for the larger company. That's networking!

The trend towards becoming more entrepreneurial are endless, and the technology trends favor it, ultimately even within larger companies.

Bottom line: Most of us want to be more entrepreneurial, to make our own decisions, and not to have to deal with a bureaucratic job or organization. We want to be rewarded for the value we add and to control our own destiny. We want to have an equity position in what we create so we can have a stake in its future and hand it down to our kids. We don't want to be EMPLOYEES!

Even so, larger organizations often still provide huge advantages in economy of scale functions, like R&D, broad distribution channels, systems, training, etc. The key is combining the best of both worlds through networking and similar organizational designs. The secret to the new networking economy is to combine the great economies of scale and mass-production capacities of the larger organizations of the past with the increasing decentralization and bottoms-up communication made possible by the information revolution. More people become entrepreneurs, but with connections and support from larger organizations, which have advantages you can't have on a small scale, including branding, research, information systems, and access to all types of products and services.

But the most critical shift is that this new economy and its organizations operate from the customer and front lines back, not from the top down, with stifling bureaucracies and fake customer service, with a computer telling you: "Hi, Mr. Dent, how can we help you? Push 1 if you are still awake, push 2 if you want to update your account, push 3 if you want to return your product, push 4 if you want to shoot us now, push 5 if you want a real person. You pushed 5, don't shoot us or hang up . . . thanks for holding, all of our agents are busy, we value your call and your business, please wait until the next agent is available . . . rinse and repeat . . ." Then you finally hang up, and you wish you could shoot them.

Yes, there are many products that can be better and cheaper with such automated computer services, which have removed the human factor along with the possibility of forever having personalized service again. But there is a better way for products and services that really matter to people, like health care and travel and financial planning.

The real opportunities revolve around developing a human browser and human server organization that is highly automated, with the best real-time, computer-generated information access and coordination delivering real-time, customized products and personalized service at lower costs.

Much of the progress and cost reduction in past decades has come from taking older, more standardized products and services and automating them through computers at the expense of personalized service. This is still the old economy—making standardized products more affordable with less and less service.

Yeah, well, I have had enough of that, although I accept it in certain areas. I want to be served by human networks, not by computer networks, which are inherently impersonal and, most of the time, are a pain in the ass to deal with. Most companies save their time and costs at the price of *your* time and costs—and it is increasingly hard to get the human advice you need when you need it without bureaucracy or waiting.

The First Solution: Direct Marketing Organizations That Get Closer to Their Customers, Know Them, and Respond More Intimately

This revolution has been taking place for decades but still has a long way to go. As I said earlier, the last 80-year revolution was about mass manufacturing and lowering costs for standardized products, thereby making them more affordable while raising the wages of the average working person, who followed standardized rules in a top-down bureaucracy. That made the first middle-class, mass-affluent economies in history, especially after World War II.

This revolution is about making marketing more direct and eliminating layers of distribution that only add costs and bureaucracy. Four new direct-marketing models have developed in recent decades:

The first is the direct producer to consumer model. This started on a larger scale with Dell computer, which began marketing directly and producing to consumer demand rather than building large inventories and pushing them through warehouses and stores. The computers were produced to order, so you didn't need big warehouses to store them. Not only does this save

Four New Direct Marketing Models

Strategy	Example
Direct Producer to Consumer	Tesla, L.L. Bean, Harry and David, Infomercials
Direct Warehouse to Consumer	Amazon, Alibaba, Best Buy, Costco
Front-line Customization	Independent Financial Planners, Concierge Doctors
Peer-to-Peer	eBay, Network Marketing, Tupperware, Uber, Airbnb

layers of costs for warehouses, retail, and bricks and mortar, but the producer interacts directly with the customers and can measure their responses and adapt more rapidly to their changing needs.

How many products are now doing the same thing: marketing through TV ads, infomercials, direct mail, and catalogues, and shipping directly from the producer to the consumer? Individuals or small groups can sell products directly to consumers over a website or through radio or TV ads. One woman sells services for helping people to build customized scrapbooks over her Internet site. She has a home office, and she turned her hobby into a prosperous and full-time business. She is direct producer to consumer.

You might be thinking this is where the network marketing model falls, but read a little further. It's more than that.

The second model is direct warehouse to consumer. This works where there are a lot of smaller-ticket and more standardized products. You need to have a big selection for these, and you still need centralized warehouses, but you don't necessarily need the retail level of consumer service. The customers know what they want. They can order one or many things, and the supplier can deliver it directly with automated service and combined shipping. Amazon and Alibaba in China are the kings of this model. But not much personal interaction here. Try to contact a real person at Amazon— good luck . . . I've tried!

Many firms market through catalogues or Internet sites, etc. They deal with and ship directly to customers, and they develop more information to better tailor their marketing and their offerings to individual customers. Think Harry & David, L.L. Bean, and Frontgate.

The big-box stores fit into this model as well. Think Walmart, Costco, Best Buy ,and Home Depot. They aren't normal, personalized retail stores. They are warehouses near you with a high selection of commodity goods, but typically with very little service. Costco doesn't even give you bags for carrying your purchases out. You have to spend a lot of time searching these giant stores; you may eventually find someone to help you, if you're lucky and search far enough.

The third model is the personal browser, for more customized products and services. This can be a customized Internet site with real people to talk to. Examples are high-end travel services; local concierge doctors or emergency-care franchises; local financial-planning firms; business consultants; lawyers; and accountants.

Here you walk in and get real, professional-level service from real people—and you don't have to wait all day to get it! If there is an ongoing relationship, you get your own personal professional, who focuses on you. Your professional browser brings you backline professional services (human servers) from their firm or from referral partners when you need them.

In this model, you will pay the most for such services. I am very happy to do that. I pay more in the arenas that most matter to me and where I want that more immediate and human service. I see this arena growing more in the decades ahead, after the direct producer-to-consumer and warehouse-to-consumer arenas max out and start to slow.

The fourth, most radical, and bottoms-up model is the peer-to-peer approach. This is about real people selling products they use and know to other people like them. Who would have thought of that?

This is where network marketing comes in. eBay is the king of this model on the Internet, along with Alibaba in China, and Amazon is rapidly following. Amazon is a combination of the direct warehouse-to-consumer and peer-to-peer model, as is Alibaba. People are selling things to other people like them over a broad and sophisticated Internet platform and website, with ratings and background checks to create trust. This has worked extremely well for commodity products from computers to sunglasses.

Airbnb is the latest innovation here, among many that are making things more personal for people to sell or share over the Internet. This is called the *sharing economy*. People are renting their bedrooms or backyard cottages or yurts or treehouses or vacation homes directly to other people over the Internet. Airbnb is now the size of a global hotel chain and is growing rapidly. At Uber, people are giving other people rides instead of paying more for taxicabs. Next will be websites for renting power tools and lawn mowers from neighbors, and similar services.

The Personal Touch

There are still, and will be, more personalized services that you want to get, more often locally, from a real person who is like you and understands the product or service—especially where you don't require a high-priced professional at exorbitant fees.

That's where network marketing—Tupperware, Avon, and companies like that—come in.

Network marketing was an example of the "new" sharing economy long before Airbnb came along. It's ultimately about people finding a product they are passionate about and actually use in their lives, and sharing it with others.

Network-marketing companies and somewhat similar models at Tupperware and Avon offer that good old-fashioned personal touch and consultation. This obviously costs more than automated online ordering. What differentiates this from the personal-browser model is that the latter approach requires someone with more specialized professional expertise, like a doctor or financial advisor or business consultant. In the peer-to-peer model, it simply requires personable and/or sales-oriented people that have a passion for a product or service and can relate and consult to people like themselves.

The New Network Model of Organization:
It's Radical and Powerful

The most powerful dimension of the computer and Internet revolution ahead will be increasingly radical changes in how we organize work, companies, allied groups of companies, and whole industries to deliver customized products and personalized service at increasingly affordable costs. The point of the new network economy is to make customization as affordable as the last revolution made standardized products. This is the most powerful and lasting theme of the coming 80-Year Four-Season Cycle.

This approach requires, first, a different way of designing and thinking about your company as a manager or entrepreneur. It requires you to see information technologies as a way to augment humans and bring affordable personalized service, not as a means in and of itself or merely as a way to reduce costs and streamline organizational bureaucracies. This is a way for front-line workers or entrepreneurs to see how they can fit into such growing networks.

Information technologies are ultimately here to *eliminate bureaucracy altogether* and even automate most of management so that *companies can organize around the customer and operate from the bottom up, not the top down*, to deliver customized products and personalized service affordably and in real time—and to make more people entrepreneurial, inside or outside of companies.

What does a network organization look like? Let me start with a real-world example today: the New York Stock Exchange. Someone runs up, rings the bell at 9:30 a.m., and runs and gets the hell out of the way. All types of chaos will follow. Zillions of trades will be made by investors, the end users. They are executed at the speed of light, and very cheaply. Everyone knows instantly what price they bought or sold at and how much money they made on a trade. Market and stock indices move up and down and all over the place, and investors can see them in real time. Then someone runs up at 4:00 and rings the bell, and the chaos stops until the next trading day.

Where's the management? Do you ever see them? Where's the bureaucracy? Who drives the system? The users! Is this a network? It certainly is NOT a top-down bureaucracy. The secret: the management, systems, rules, and bureaucracy are automated in the software, which operates at the speed of light and around the customers, from the bottom up.

Why is this not more common in more organizations? Because this system is pure information—no hard products or raw materials. But all products are becoming more information-intensive. This model will grow in the decades ahead and will transform our economy and organizations—especially government, which is service- and information-intensive.

I spend 15 pages on this in chapter 8 of *The Demographic Cliff,* which is aimed more at corporate managers, but here's the Cliff Notes for you as a potential entrepreneur to understand how these changes will emerge and affect you over time:

1. Start with the customer. Define your company's products or services in terms of the benefits and the real results that customers receive.
2. Break your customers into the smallest practical segments that have substantially different needs.
3. Create the smallest teams of skills that offer front-line human "browsers" who can focus on the needs of each unique customer segment. This is how you begin to create real, human, personalized service. Multifunctional and people-oriented skills are valued here. Every customer group gets its own concierge!

4. Take as much information on the customer and your products and costs as possible to the front lines by putting such information, rules, and expertise into software that is accessible by these front-line teams. Make as many decisions as possible on the front lines!

5. For the human functions that require too much specialized expertise or economies of scale to put on the front lines: organize them into backline human "servers." These people are available as much as possible in real time to back up and assist the front-line browsers. They don't deal with the customers directly unless this is facilitated by the front-line browser teams.

6. Management no longer consists of bosses and second-guessers. Management defines the strategic focus of the company: who we are and what we deliver in real results for the customer. Management develops measures for those results at all levels. It also defines fair costs that the front-line browsers pay for the services of the backline servers, just like outside consultants.

7. Design and orchestrate the network organization. You are not only strategic visionaries and leaders, but judge and jury. There will be disputes between browsers and servers or customers and browsers. You have to resolve them fairly.

8. Perhaps most importantly: make every front-line browser and backline server team a real business. That means allocating fixed and variable costs to all teams; it also means measuring not just their success at creating tangible results for customers, but their bottom-line profit. Software increasingly allows you to do this. Design software likewise to determine the profitability of every customer and/ or customer segment.

This network organization is likely to determine the winners and losers in the years and decades ahead. It will allow more and more employees to become entrepreneurs within the company or spin off outside, becoming much more effective and accountable.

However you design your business and career, *you want to find ways to network or affiliate with the larger companies that are moving towards this network model.*

Most people don't realize that General Motors ultimately beat out Ford as the number-one car company from the early 1930s onward as a result of its superior organization. It was this company, through the venerable Alfred Sloan, that pioneered the last new organizational model. Ford pioneered the Model T and the assembly line—both huge technological and organizational achievements. But GM redesigned the entire organization, with cost and marketing advantages that could not be rivaled—as did General Electric, even more so, after World War II.

As I observed in chapters 1 and 3, I think a global slowdown should favor the networking model more than others, as more people look to make extra income or create a part- or full-time business that they can control and rely on more than a job in an environment of job shock and the highest unemployment we will see in our lifetimes.

In the last chapter I will look at the classic options for becoming an entrepreneur, because this is the time do it if you ever do. I will look at the pros and cons of the four basic options for becoming your own business. I will share my insights into strategies from my decade of consulting to entrepreneurial companies in the 1980s and early 1990s—before I wrote *The Great Boom Ahead* and became an economist and started my own business.

Chapter Six

Options for Becoming an Entrepreneur in this Opportune Decade Ahead
The Pros and Cons

As I have stated many times in this book, entrepreneurs thrive in challenging times and down economies. Most people and companies do well in booms. The downturns separate the wheat from the chaff. In chapter 5, I showed that the whole economy is going to become more entrepreneurial for decades to come, as even larger companies have to become networks of smaller and more accountable businesses within—browser and server teams.

You might even call this the "entrepreneurial century." But the people that will reap the greatest rewards and prosper in the difficult transition to this new network and entrepreneurial economy will be the people that become their own businesses now! Even better if you can be your own business and hook up or network with a larger company that has major advantages you can't create on your own. After all, we aren't on *Little House on the Prairie* any more.

In this chapter, I will look at the advantages and disadvantages of the different ways of becoming your own business. In addition to my primary mission of promoting better economic education and forecasting for everyday people and businesses, I am a strong promoter of people becoming entrepreneurs for higher self-fulfillment, more control over their destiny, and getting a higher percentage of the value-added generated versus most jobs. *The key is to find the strategy and model that best fit your skills, risk capacity, and financial resources.*

Here's a brief summation of the typical paths to becoming an entrepreneur. I look at these as any good economist would: what are the risks versus the potential returns? You have to consider both, and that's where the differences come. You could potentially succeed at any of these models. It's up to you to judge which model fits your personal aspirations, risk tolerance, temperament and skills.

1. The Franchise Model

PROS: This model has the highest chance of success and hence has a low risk of failure, as the system is proven in many markets across a country or region. Most of these companies are very good at using demographic and lifestyle analysis to target areas that will have the customer base to ensure that you succeed. And of course you get all types of advertising and marketing support and management training and systems. The corporate HQ provides the scale factors and systems; you provide the local finance and management. But there are an array of concepts: more broad-based or more niche, earlier-stage and less proven, or more mature and very proven. So the odds of success and risk do vary and that gives you more choices to fit your risk profile.

This option is very popular among sports stars and celebrities, who have a lot of cash and want to diversify. It is also good for investors with higher net worth, who want more predictable returns for retirement. I have met a few extended families that pitched in and built a small or large empire of franchises. A good strategy for that is to start with a few and then use the profits from those to buy and build more.

CONS: The big challenge for this great and proven option is simple: you already have to be rich to get richer. Typically you have to put up anywhere from

$100,000 to $1 million to buy the franchise. Then there are start-up costs on top of that.

The other disadvantage I see for this model is that it has succeeded so well from the greatest boom in history and the aging of the baby boom. But going forward, most restaurants, dry cleaners, and other concepts in this arena are going to be past their peak in spending. That means you are going to pay a premium price for many franchises that are going to grow much more slowly or even decline. I saw an article about how major chains like Burger King are already growing more slowly than they used to. What happens when an economic decline makes people less likely to eat out or to become much more price-sensitive?

2. Start Your Own Business

PROS: With this approach, you get to design exactly what you want to do around what you are best at. You can often start in a small location or out of your home and only commit more investment and time as your business proves itself. I've been on stage with a speaker named Loral Langemeier, who trains people on how to turn their hobby or whatever they already do for free into a business (like the scrapbook lady I mentioned earlier). Loral stresses making cash flow right from the beginning—a great concept. Many people start restaurants, bars, tailoring and alteration shops, dry cleaners, laundromats, computer services, hair salons, flower shops, yoga centers, clothing stores, and so on. Demographically, I would choose the laundromats to benefit from up-and-coming millennials, and yoga studios and flower shops to track the aging baby boomers.

My strongest recommendation to all such everyday entrepreneurs is to spend as little money as possible until you have proven your concept. Rent, don't buy equipment or facilities; don't hire a secretary or buy a lot of furniture. Keep your day job, and do your business on the side until you quit that job and source of cash flow. If you do start making profits, keep putting a little aside along the way to get you through rainy days. These are inevitable now that you and not your employer is at risk.

CONS: You are taking more risk to become your own boss, but often the rewards are not higher or not much higher than those an equivalent job. Many such local stores or businesses end up pay you something like a normal salary, although they take longer hours. You also have to deal with petty things you don't enjoy, like accounting, taxes, and local regulations.

But the biggest disadvantage here is that the failure rates are far higher than most people assume: 80 percent within five years, according to the statistics I last saw. I watch most of the restaurants in my area that are not proven franchises fall like flies. One failed in three weeks; another took four months. Most take a few years. A few survive past that. To start a small restaurant, you have to commit to a one-year-plus lease, and you have to invest money and/or borrow to buy equipment and furniture. People often put their life's savings into the business, or they borrow money from relatives or friends. If the business fails (and it often does), you lose your savings, and maybe damage some close relationships—bad karma, as they say.

3. Start a Radically New Business That Has Very High Growth and Profit Potential

PROS: This is the American entrepreneurial dream. This is *apparently* the most fulfilling path. This is what most people would love to do. These are the people that make the magazine covers when they succeed big-time. Don't just have your own business and be your own boss: be all that you can be, be a multimillionaire or billionaire, a mini Steve Jobs, or maybe even a Steve Jobs. In network marketing, be one of the top producers that makes millions a year. This requires doing something that is unique or different, that is radical and often not proven. Or, better, it takes finding a concept that has already been proven on a smaller scale and duplicating and expanding it regionally, nationally or globally. Since it's often not proven, it means experimenting and testing and refining and adapting until you get the recipe right. This can take years. In his book *Outliers*, Malcolm Gladwell shows how it typically takes 10,000 hours of immersion in a new skill or process before you master it. That's five years, if you do it full-time—and that doesn't include the time to market it and prove it in new markets after that. So double that or more. It took me about eight years to get my first breakthrough, write my first book, and start my first newsletter, but I did it in about two-thirds time, so that's right on his 10,000 hours. For the other third, I consulted to small businesses to pay the bills. I love Malcolm: he brings simple, breakthrough concepts and proves how predictable things are!

If you do something proven and are doing it on your own, a franchise or large-chain company is very likely going to beat you with superior financing, management, systems, and scale for lower costs. The rewards can be huge if you can prove a new concept and expand or duplicate it to the point that you can sell it for a high multiple of earnings or go public or bring in management over time. You can step out more and more, and you can have growing residual income with less time involved, and ultimately maybe none.

CONS: This is the highest-risk option by far. The process of endless experimentation can be very stressful and frustrating. You're most often on your own with no guide, no model to duplicate, no one to help you do something that typically hasn't been done before. This is the model I chose, and frankly at many points I have questioned whether the returns were worth the risks. Suffice it to say that it's not always as great as it sounds.

I definitely don't recommend this path to most people. It is the loneliest path until it becomes proven, and that takes much longer when you are going against the grain. The predictability of growth and earnings is very low and very volatile. You never know when you are going to have a bigger setback than you expected and you can't cover your expenses—so have some reserves and don't be overoptimistic. In fact, one of the biggest reasons for failure is that the radical entrepreneurs fall in love with their own baby and think the world is going to come running. They spend most of their money or seed capital from investors on aggressive marketing, but the customers don't come running. Then you're out of money, and then no one wants to invest in you again, or only if you give up much more of your equity.

To me, the worst part about this option is that if you do have to raise substantial investment (which is likely at some point), the chances are very high you will fail altogether and your investors, who could be friends and family, lose everything. That really hurts! If you invest your own money or take on loans and you fail, you could go bankrupt. I heard once that the typical major entrepreneur that ultimately makes it big, goes bankrupt four times first. Ouch!

So here I offer the same advice as to the everyday entrepreneur, but more so: do this part-time at first; don't give up your job. Minimize expenses and commitments until you really prove the concept and have an expandable business model. Test, test, test ... everything in small doses before you make larger expenditures or investments. Rent, don't buy wherever possible. The biggest challenges tend to come in marketing—getting that first customer—rather than in the technology or product-prototype development, so don't underestimate the expense and efforts that are likely to be required for marketing and spend that money wisely.

Finally, I get to network marketing.

4. Network Marketing

PROS: The three biggest advantages to network marketing should be more obvious than most people see. The first is that, like a franchise, you are getting branding, marketing, and sales support and tools, training, and systems. You get the economy of scale of a larger company or network. The second is that, as with starting your own business, you can do this one step at a time, part-time at first, without quitting your job or business, and you can commit more as you prove more results. The third is that it requires very little up-front investment—that's the biggest advantage compared to the other options. You don't have a franchise fee, you don't have to lease a store-front or buy (or borrow to finance) a lot of equipment; typically you just have to have some inventory and training materials and some inventory. Unlike with the three options above, if you try this and it fails, you don't lose your ass. Furthermore, the risks of loss if things don't work out are the lowest by far of the four options here.

This is also a fulfilling profession. You choose a product or service that you already love and have an affinity for, but you don't have to go it alone, as you do when starting your own product or service. It is a people business; it is a part of the sharing economy and the peer-to-peer direct marketing model I discussed in chapter 5. You get to confer with other like-minded people once or twice a year if you choose. You get to meet people you prospect to. If you do build a downline, you have a family of entrepreneurs. If people under you do succeed with your help, that is gratifying and profitable. If they fail, they don't lose their ass and you don't have to feel bad about it. If you do succeed, the potential profits are enormous, where they typically aren't if you just start the normal local business.

There is another advantage to this industry. Recruiting people into your downline actually becomes easier when the economy is slowing and people are losing jobs or are being downshifted into part-time jobs. In the great recession of 2008–09, direct-selling distributors actually went up 6 percent, while retail sales went down 5 percent, as this chart shows.

Direct Sellers Outperform in Recession Like 2008–2009
Number of Direct Selling Distributors vs. Retail Sales, U.S.

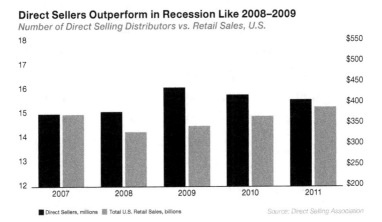

■ Direct Sellers, millions ▨ Total U.S. Retail Sales, billions   *Source: Direct Selling Association*

CONS: Only 10 percent or so ultimately succeed to some degree part-time, and only 1 percent make it big full-time. That's the clear disadvantage of this model. Many promoters of this industry preach the dream, but they don't communicate what it really takes to succeed. I see that changing in the best companies. The chances of success are lower than in the three options above, but that's what a rational person should expect, given that the investment risks and up-front commitment are so low.

I look at the unique dynamics of the network marketing industry more just ahead.

Network-Marketing Profits Are
Highly Skewed to the 1 Percent

From statistics from a few very large companies in network marketing that have to report their financial data, here is how the picture looks to me as an objective outsider: 87 percent of the commissions tend to go to the top 1 percent of distributors, who obviously tend to be full-time entrepreneurs.

Hey, in the U.S., as of 2014, nearly 50 percent of the wealth goes to the top 1 percent. So this is already a reality of life. But 87 percent to the top 1 percent—that is even more skewed than normal.

The rest goes to nearly 10 percent, who sell minor amounts of product part-time. So 10–11 percent make all of the money, and 1 percent make most of that. The other 89 percent or so end up being customers who buy regularly and are happy with the product. No one invests any substantial money here, and no one really loses much. But the great majority of people don't achieve the dream of becoming a multimillionaire entrepreneurs working out of their homes.

Why is the model for network marketing profitable, and why has it been growing for decades? It is very simple: the industry draws in a lot of aspirants through its distributors (a big net) who have potential incentives to bring them in, but they end up finding 1–10 percent (the tunas) that drive the revenues and profits for the company and the distributors that do sell. That's why I agree with Carl Icahn, who says this is an industry that should continue to grow, and not with Bill Ackman, who says that it is more of a Ponzi scheme.

Before I wrote this book, I had met over a dozen individuals or couples who were making millions a year in commissions, so they were multimillionaires and beyond. Many were met at Tony Robbins' Platinum Group conferences, where you have to be a very successful entrepreneur just to afford to get in. I spoke at a network-marketing association conference in Dallas, where I met several people who had 500,000 to 1 million people under them in their downlines. That was unimaginable to me!

Clearly the Dream Is Achievable, but . . .

The million-dollar question to me is, what is the difference between the people who do make it big and the many who get minor gains at best? (By the way, I have met many people who get only minor, part-time income, but almost all of them have felt that they still got a lot of education and motivation from their involvement. I haven't seen many complaints, unlike Bernie Madoff investors, who were involved in a true Ponzi scheme.)

If I had to put the answer in one sentence for this profession I would say: it is the people who are serious about building a real business that succeed, as is the case in any entrepreneurial option. But of course, there is more to it than acknowledging the risks already taken.

To summarize: You need to seriously consider which of these four options best suits your skills, aspirations, and risk tolerance. Then you need to pick a sector of the economy or markets that you understand and in which can add value for your customers. You need to consider which sectors of your markets will benefit from the two largest trends: (1) the continued aging of the larger baby-boom generation, and (2) the emergence of the up-and-coming millennial generation. Finally, you need to understand the skills you will need to succeed in the choice you make. You will either have to acquire them yourself or hire or partner with someone (or with another company) who has the skills you don't.

For people who want to keep up with what I am thinking, I have a free newsletter, *Economy and Markets*, at harrydent.com/newsletter.

For people who have a serious business with numbers of employees and strong growth prospects, you will want to consider my in-depth, interactive nine-CD program called *Business Strategies for the Winter Season*. This is available at dentresearch.com.

Epilogue

How to Protect Your Wealth
Once You've Made It

There is a famous saying among financial advisors and professionals who work with wealth management: "It's often easier to build wealth than it is to keep it."

Success breeds complacency... and many times a propensity to take higher risks. However, that is usually not the best thing to do. Becoming an entrepreneur almost always increases your risk, so why add to that?

Now you *are* your business. If it fails, *you* fail. If it goes through a strong down cycle, *you* go through that cycle. Employees are usually protected from those cycles, because the employers and owners absorb more of the shock. You may not get a raise, but unless you're laid off, you'll still have your health care and wages. Today, though, being laid off is a real risk for an employee; it's job shock, and there will be a lot of that in the worsening winter season ahead.

I am offering you three simple principles of advice in this epilogue, as I don't have time here to cover a full range of investment strategies (as I do in *Zero Hour*).

1. When you build significant cash and cash flow as an entrepreneur, take some of that cash flow to invest, diversifying your wealth and keeping a stash for rainy days.

2. As in any business, don't lose sight of your core competence—don't stray as a result of your success into businesses or investments you don't understand.

3. Understand in this winter season that the range of investments is limited, because bubbles are bursting everywhere and having devastating, long-term impacts.

Diversify Risks and Have a Security Bucket

I often speak at global events for Tony Robbins' Platinum Group. Participants are very successful entrepreneurs, who often have made a lot of money in a relatively short time. Tony has a multiday event once a year during which he comprehensively discusses financial planning and wealth building.

The most important takeaway from my own experience is that he advises segmenting your wealth into different buckets: *security*, *growth*, and *dream*. In my history and in the history of most entrepreneurs with whom I have worked, it's the security bucket that is missing.

I am a risk taker. When I was successful, I used to put all of my cash flow into other risky investments—no security bucket. That strategy caused me unnecessary periods of financial stress. I wish had had heard Tony's viewpoint before I made my first small fortune. Not having a substantial security bucket of safe investments is insane when you are already largely or fully in a high-risk entrepreneurial business.

One large network marketing distributor told me he heard similar advice from finance author Robert Kiyosaki during a major conference on network marketing. Robert told the audience that once they have made it, they should invest a substantial amount of cash flow and wealth in less risky investments to diversify their wealth.

While you're protecting your wealth and saving for a rainy day, continue to focus totally on your business; continue succeeding! Entrepreneurial success typically requires continual work, and complacency is your worst enemy. It is typically best to invest in passive investments through a financial advisor, so you don't take time from your focus on continuing to build your business. But as Tony said, diversify your risk and have safer assets for rainy days, as you will almost certainly have down times as an entrepreneur.

Stay Focused on Your Core Competence

Another great presentation I wish I had heard before I had my first surge of cash flow and wealth was a talk given by entrepreneur Keith Cunningham. Keith had built a multimillion-dollar business but then used that wealth to enter into other ventures that he didn't fully understand—and he lost most of it. He refocused on his core competence and built that wealth back the hard way.

I had the same experience. I built multimillions of dollars in wealth in the late 1990s and early 2000s when my very successful contrarian forecasts generated from massive book and speaking revenues, and from an investment fund I subadvised. What seemed so natural at the time ended up being naïve.

Here's what I was thinking: "I started my own business and have consulted to many more. I am good at predicting new trends. My cash flow and wealth keep building way beyond my needs. I should take my wealth and excess cash flow and invest it in other entrepreneurs and new ventures that can change the world in the same meaningful way I did!"

Note that changing the world means employing the most radical innovation, which has the highest chance of failure.

I was adding high-risk businesses to my own high-risk business! That is nuts!

I staked almost all of my net worth on fifteen new ventures. Only two of them are standing today— the only ones that closely fit my core competence and in which I had substantial involvement. Yes, one of those may make back all my losses or more, but that is still to be seen.

The only businesses I have solidly made a lot of money from were the ones I built myself, in areas in which I had unique competence, skills, and experience. I am currently working on a new vision that fits my unique insights, but with partners who can execute the vision, as I cannot afford to take time away from my main forecasting and newsletter business.

Investing passively and at lower risk with part of your growing wealth and cash flow is principle number 1. If you are going to start another business or two, only do it in areas that strongly fit your core competence, and don't do it if the time it will require threatens the success of your present cash cow. That's principle number 2. Principle number 3 is to understand this once-in-a-lifetime winter season's unique challenges for investment.

The Winter Season Greatly Narrows
Investment Options: Tread Carefully

At Dent Research, we go beyond reporting demographic trends and cycles. We also include the critical insight that you must have a different business and investment strategy for each season of our economy. You and your business have your own seasons and cycles ... but the larger economy affects and often overrides your cycles.

As I discussed in chapter 4, we saw a classic fall bubble-boom season from 1983 to 2007. In fact, that season produced the greatest and most global boom in modern history, and it was driven by the massive baby boom around the world as well as by the personal-computer and Internet revolution.

All fall booms have to deleverage and consolidate in the survival-of-the-fittest winter season to prepare for the next spring boom. From an investment point of view, that means almost all investments fall dramatically and come back down to earth.

There is nowhere to hide. Only cash-equivalent investments and the safest government and corporate bonds do well. Stocks around the world, real estate, commodities, junk bonds—all of the risk assets get killed. That narrows the options.

This means most asset-allocation plans for diversification that typical stockbrokers recommend (which do well in a boom) will fail. Diversification doesn't work when everything goes down.

Most financial advisors will tell you to stay invested for the long term: stocks and real estate always go up. That's just not the case in this unique winter season, which occurs only once in a lifetime. The worst crashes in all areas tend to occur in the winter season, and it often takes decades—not years—for stocks, real estate, and commodities to get back to their peaks.

For these reasons, you must preserve your capital and be in the safest areas. Into the next danger zone, these areas are cash equivalents, like short-term T-bills and CDs, and the highest-quality, longer-term government and corporate bonds. If you want to take some risk, use a minority portion of your portfolio to bet that stocks and other risk assets will go down, a process known as *going short*.

When there is a major crash, as there was back in 2008 into early 2009, then you can buy in the best demographic sectors. By 2020–22, you should be able to invest for the longer term in a more diversified portfolio, but it should be weighted more toward emerging-country stocks and sectors like health care in the developed countries.

I have a free daily newsletter at www.harrydent .com/newsletter that allows you to keep informed on our unique economic views and investment strategies—and get to know us better.

About the Author

Harry S. Dent, Jr. is the founder of Dent Research, an economic-research firm specializing in demographic trends. His mission is "helping people understand change."

Using exciting new research developed from years of hands-on business experience, Mr. Dent offers unprecedented and refreshingly understandable tools for seeing the key economic trends that will affect your life, your business, and your investments over the rest of your lifetime.

Mr. Dent is also a best-selling author. In his book *The Great Boom Ahead* (1992), he stood virtually alone in accurately forecasting the unanticipated boom of the 1990s and the continued expansion into 2007. In his recent book, *The Demographic Cliff* (2014), he continued to educate audiences about his predictions for the next great depression, which he has been forecasting now for twenty years. Mr. Dent is the editor of *The Economy and Markets*, *Boom-and-bust*, and *The Leading Edge* newsletters, and he is the creator of the Dent Network.

Mr. Dent received his MBA from Harvard Business School, where he was a Baker Scholar and was elected to the Century Club for leadership excellence. At Bain & Company, he was a strategy consultant for Fortune 100 companies. He has also been the CEO of several entrepreneurial-growth companies and has been a new-venture investor. Since 1988, he has been speaking to executives and investors around the world. He has appeared on *Good Morning America*, PBS, CNBC, CNN, and Fox and has been featured in *Barron's*, *Investor's Business Daily*, *Entrepreneur*, *Fortune*, *SUCCESS*, *U.S. News and World Report*, *Business Week*, *The Wall Street Journal*, *American Demographics*, *Gentlemen's Quarterly*, and *Omni*.